Practice in Daily Life 20

생활 속의 참선수행 시리즈

The Secret to Living Without Fear

겁내지 않고 당당하게

한마음

hanmaum

겁내지 않고 당당하게

생활 속의 참선수행 시리즈 20 (한영합본)
대행큰스님 법문

발행일 2026년 1월 1판 1쇄

영문번역 한마음국제문화원

표지디자인 박수연

편집 한마음국제문화원

발행 한마음출판사

출판등록 384-2000-000010

전화 031-470-3175

팩스 031-470-3209

이메일 onemind@hanmaum.org

The Secret to Living Without Fear

Practice in Daily Life 20
Dharma Talks by Seon Master Daehaeng

First Edition, First Printing, January 2026
English Translation by Hanmaum International Culture Institute
Edited by Hanmaum International Culture Institute
Cover Design by Su Yeon Park
Published by Hanmaum Publications
www.hanmaumbooks.org

Printed in the Republic of Korea

ISBN 978-89-91857-72-8
ISBN 978-89-91857-50-6 (세트)

차례

CONTENTS

내 한생각에 일체가 움직이리라

천지 만물 모든 생명

너와 함께 있으니

유정 무정 화합하여

한마음을 이루면

언제 어디서나

내 몸 아님이 없나니

모든 것 내 한생각에

움직이리라

The Power of a Single Thought

All beings and everything in the world
are all together with me.
If I can combine the seen and unseen,
and become one mind,
then wherever I go,
everything I meet,
everyone I meet,
is also my body.
And from this all-together-place,
the thoughts I give rise to move everything.

부처와 더불어

일체 만생과 만물은

모두가 공했으니

공하여 평등하면

열반이자 부처요,

한생각을 냈다 하면

그대로가 법이며

움직이는 용이라.

All the Buddhas,
and every life and thing,
are all empty,
ceaselessly changing, and interacting.
When I truly realize this,
and know that everything is myself,
this is nirvana,
this is Buddha.
And from this state,
a single thought will become reality,
a single thought will move and work
across the entire world.

머리글

대행큰스님이 지난 50여 년 동안 끊임없이 중생들에게 베풀어 주신 수많은 법문이 있었지만, 핵심을 짚어 내는 하나의 단어가 있다면, 그건 아마도 "참나"일 것입니다. 항상 나와 함께 있어서 보지 못하는 내 안의 진짜 나, 그 "참나"를 발견하여 당당하고 싱그럽게 살아가기를 바라는, 중생을 위한 스님의 간절한 바람은 이 한 편의 법문 속에도 여지없이 드러나 있습니다.

누구에게나 내면에는 만물만생을 다 먹여 살리고도 되남는 마음속 한 점의 불씨가 있습니다. 그 영원한 불씨를 찾아 광대무변한 마음법의 이치를 체득하여, 진정한 자유인으로서, 우주의 한 일원으로서 당당히 그 역할을 해나가길 바라는 대행큰스님의 간곡한 뜻이 이 법문을 통해 여러분 모두의 마음에 전해지길 바랍니다.

한마음국제문화원 일동 합장

Foreword

For over fifty years, Daehaeng Kun Sunim gave countless Dharma talks and teachings to beings without number, but if all those talks could be summed up into one word, it would be "true self."

This true essence has always been with us, yet remains unseen. Discover it for yourself, and in doing so, learn to live with courage, dignity, and joy. That all beings should awaken to this true essence was Daehaeng Kun Sunim's deepest wish. When you've tasted the most refreshing spring water imaginable, you naturally want to share it with others.

Within us all is this seed, this spark that feeds and sustains each and every being. Discover this eternal spark and realize its profound and unlimited ability. If you can do this, you'll know what it means to truly be a free person, and you can fulfill the great role that is yours as a member of the whole universe.

With palms together,
The Hanmaum International Culture Institute

대행큰스님에 대하여

대행큰스님께서는 여러 면에서 매우 보기 드문 선사禪師셨다. 무엇보다 선사라면 당연히 비구 스님을 떠올리는 전통 속에서 여성으로서 선사가 되셨으며, 비구 스님들을 제자로 두었던 유일한 비구니 스님이셨고, 노년층 여성이 주된 신도계층을 이루었던 한국 불교에 젊은 세대의 청장년층 남녀들을 대거 참여하게 만들어 한국불교에 새로운 풍격風格을 일으키는 데 일조한 큰 스승이셨다. 또한 전통 비구니 강원과 비구니 종단에 대한 지속적인 지원을 펼치심으로써 비구니 승단을 발전시키는 데 중추적인 역할을 하셨다.

About Daehaeng Kun Sunim

Daehaeng *Kun Sunim*[1](1927 - 2012) was a rare teacher in Korea: a female *Seon*(Zen)[2] master, a nun whose students also included monks, and a teacher who helped revitalize Korean Buddhism by dramatically increasing the participation of young people and men.

---

1. Sunim / Kun Sunim: Sunim is the respectful title of address for a Buddhist monk or nun in Korea, and Kun Sunim is the title given to outstanding nuns or monks.

2. Seon(禪)(Chan, Zen): Seon describes the unshakeable state where one has firm faith in their inherent foundation, their Buddha-nature, and so returns everything they encounter back to this fundamental mind. It also means letting go of "I," "me," and "mine" throughout one's daily life.

큰스님께서는 어느 누구나 마음수행을 통해 깨달을 수 있음을 강조하시면서 삭발 제자와 유발 제자를 가리지 않고 법을 구하는 이들에게는 모두 똑같이 가르침을 주셨다.

스님은 1927년 서울에서 태어나 일찍이 9세경에 자성을 밝히셨고, 당신이 증득證得하신 바를 완성하기 위해 오랫동안 산중에서 수행하셨다. 훗날, 누더기가 다 된 해진 옷을 걸치고 손에 주어지는 것만을 먹으며 지냈던 그 당시를 회상하며 스님은 의도적으로 고행을 하고자 했던 것이 아니라 당신에게 주어진 환경이 그러했노라고, 또한 근본 불성 자리에 일체를 맡기고 그 맡긴 일이 어떻게 작용하는지를 관하는 일에 완전히 몰두하고 있었기에 다른 것에는 신경을 쓸 틈이 없었노라고 말씀하셨다.

그 시절의 체험이 스님의 가르치는 방식을 형성하는데 깊은 영향을 미쳤다. 스님은 우리가 본래부터 어마어마한 잠재력을, 무궁무진한 에너지와 지혜를 가지고 있는데도 대부분이 그 역량을 알지 못해 끊임없이 많은 고통을 겪으며 살고 있음을 절실히 느끼며 안타까워하셨다. 우리들 각자 안에 존재하는 이 위대한 빛을 명백히 알고 있었

She broke out of traditional models of spiritual practice to teach in such a way that allowed anyone to practice and awaken, making laypeople a particular focus of her efforts. At the same time, she was a major force for the advancement of *Bhikkunis,*[3] heavily supporting traditional nuns' colleges as well as the modern Bhikkuni Council of Korea.

Born in Seoul, Korea, she awakened when she was around eight years old and spent the years that followed learning to put her understanding into practice. For years, she wandered the mountains of Korea, wearing ragged clothes and eating only what was at hand. Later, she explained that she hadn't been pursuing some type of asceticism; rather, she was just completely absorbed

---

3. Bhikkunis: Female sunims who are fully ordained are called Bhikkuni (比丘尼) sunims, while male sunims who are fully ordained are called Bhikku (比丘) sunims. This can also be a polite way of indicating male or female sunims.

기에, 스님은 본래부터 가지고 있는 근본자성自性인 '참나'를 믿고 의지해 살라 가르치셨고, 이 중요한 진리에서 벗어나는 그 어떤 것도 가르치기를 단호히 거부하셨다.

의도한 바는 아니셨지만, 스님은 매일매일의 일상 속에서 누구나 내면에 갖추어 가지고 있는 근본이자 진수眞髓인 참나와 진정으로 통할 수 있게 되었을 때 어떠한 일이 일어나는지를 역력히 보여 주셨다. 사람들은 스님 곁에 있을 때 자신들을 무한히 받아 주고 품어 주는 것만 같은, 말로 형언키 어려운 정밀靜謐한 기운을 느꼈고, 스님이 다른 사람들을 도와줄 때 드러내 보이는 깊은 법력 또한 목도하곤 하였다. 하지만, 이 모든 일들은 당신 자신을 돋보이게 하거나 과시하려 했던 게 아니었다. 사실 스님께서는 당신의 법력을 늘 감추려고 하셨다. 마음공부의 목적이 놀라운 능력을 갖게 되는 것이 아님에도 대중들이 그것에만 집착하게 되는 폐단을 우려하셨기 때문이었다.

그렇지만 당신이 하신 모든 일을 통해, 우리가 내면에 있는 근본과 진정으로 하나가 되었을 때 그 능력과 자유로움이 어떤 것인지를 보여주셨다. 스님은 우리 모두가 근본을 통해 연결되어 있으므로 다 통할 수 있고, 그럼으로

in entrusting everything to her fundamental Buddha essence and observing how that affected her life.

Those years profoundly shaped Kun Sunim's later teaching style; she intimately knew the great potential, energy, and wisdom inherent within each of us, and recognized that most of the people she encountered suffered because they didn't realize this about themselves. Seeing clearly the great light in every individual, she taught people to rely upon this inherent foundation, and refused to teach anything that distracted from this most important truth.

Without any particular intention to do so, Daehaeng Kun Sunim demonstrated on a daily basis the freedom and ability that arise when we truly connect with this fundamental essence inherent within us.

The sense of acceptance and connection people felt from being around her, as well as the

써 서로 깊이 이해할 수 있다는 것을 보여 주셨으며, 더 나아가 우리가 근본자리에서 일으키는 한생각이 이 세상에 법이 되어 돌아갈 수 있다는 것도 보여 주셨다.

어떤 의미에서는 이 모든 일이 우리가 만물만생과 정말로 하나가 되었을 때 자연스레 부수적으로 나오는 것이라고 할 수 있다. 상대를 둘로 보거나 방해물로 여기는 마음이 사라졌을 때, 진정으로 모두와 조화롭게 흘러갈 수 있게 되었을 때 이 모든 일이 가능할 수 있게 되는 것이다. 이렇게 되면, 다가오는 상대가 누구든 별개의 존재로 느끼지 않게 된다. 그들이 또 다른 우리 자신들의 모습이기 때문이다. 일체가 둘이 아님을 뼛속 깊이 느끼는 사람이, 어찌 자신 앞에 닥친 인연을 나 몰라라 하고 등져 버릴 수 있겠는가?

스님은 중생들이 가지고 오는 어려운 문제나 상황들을 해결할 수 있도록 도와주셨으며, 이러한 스님의 자비로운 원력은 당신이 도시로 나와 본격적으로 대중들을 가르치기 이전에 이미 한국에서는 전설이 되어 있었다. 1950년대 말경, 치악산 상원사 근처 한 움막에서 수행차 몇 년간 머무르신 적이 있었는데, 그 소문을 듣고 전국에

abilities she manifested, weren't things she was trying to show off. In fact, she usually tried to hide those because people would tend to cling to them, not realizing that chasing after these cannot lead to either freedom or awakening.

Nonetheless, in her very life, in everything she did, she was an example of the true freedom and wisdom that arise from this very basic, fundamental essence that we all have – that we are. She showed that because we are all interconnected, we can deeply understand what's going on with others, and that the intentions we give rise to can manifest and function in the world.

All of these are, in a sense, side effects, things that arise naturally when we are truly one with everyone and everything around us. They happen because we are able to flow in harmony with our world, with no dualistic views or attachments to get in the way. At this point, other beings are not cut off from us; they are another aspect

서 찾아오는 사람들이 끊이질 않았다. 차마 그들의 고통스러운 호소를 내칠 수가 없었던 스님은 일일이 그들의 말에 귀 기울이며 마음을 다해 그들을 도와주셨다. 스님은 자비를 물 마른 웅덩이에서 죽어 가는 물고기를 살리는 방생에 비유하셨다. 집세가 없어 셋집에서 쫓겨난 사람들에게 집을 마련해 주고, 학비가 없어서 학교를 마칠 수 없는 학생들에게 학비를 대주셨지만, 스님의 자비행慈悲行을 아는 사람은 손에 꼽을 정도밖에 되지 않았다.

그러나 문제를 해결해 주면 그때뿐 또 다른 문제가 닥쳐오면 속수무책이 되어 버리고 마는 사람들을 보며, 스님께서는 중생들이 자신의 문제를 스스로 해결하고 **윤회輪廻**[1]의 굴레에서 벗어나 자유인이 될 수 있는 도리를 가르치는 일이 더 시급함을 느끼셨다. 누구나가 다 가지고 있는 '참나', 이 내면의 밝디밝은 진수眞髓를 알게 하여, 자신들이 자유롭게 사는 것은 물론이요, 자신들의 삶이 인연

---

1. 윤회(輪廻): 산스크리트의 삼사라(samsara)를 번역한 말로 쉼 없이 돈다는 생사의 바퀴를 뜻함. 다시 말해, 수레바퀴가 끊임없이 구르는 것과 같이, 중생이 번뇌와 업에 의하여 삼계(三界: 색계, 욕계, 무색계) 육도(六道: 지옥, 아귀, 축생, 아수라, 인간, 천상)라는 생사의 세계를 그치지 않고 돌고 도는 현상을 일컬음.

of ourselves. Who, feeling this to their very bones, could turn their back on others?

It was this deep compassion that made her a legend in Korea long before she formally started teaching. She was known for having the spiritual power to help people in all circumstances and with every kind of problem. She compared compassion to freeing a fish from a drying puddle, putting a homeless family into a home, or providing the school fees that would allow a student to finish high school. And when she did things like this, and more, few knew that she was behind it.

Her compassion was also unconditional. She would offer what help she could to individuals and organizations, whether they be Christian or Buddhist, a private organization or governmental. She would help nuns' temples that had no relationship with her temple, Christian organizations that looked after children living on their own, city-run projects to help care for the elderly,

맺은 모든 이에게 축복이 되어 이 한세상을 활달히 살아갈 수 있도록 해야겠다고 다짐하셨다.

마침내 산에서 내려온 스님께서는 1972년 경기도 안양에 한마음선원을 설립하셨다. 이후 40여 년 동안 한마음선원에 주석하시며, 지혜를 원하는 자에게 지혜를, 배고프고 가난한 자에게는 먹을 것과 물질을, 아파하는 자에게는 치유의 방편을 내어 주시는 무한량의 자비를 베푸시며 불법의 진리를 가르쳐 주셨다.

스님은 도움이 필요한 다양한 사회복지 프로그램을 후원하셨고, 6개국에 9개의 국외 지원과 국내 15개의 지원을 세우셨다. 또한 스님의 가르침은 영어, 독일어, 스페인어, 러시아어, 중국어, 일본어, 불어, 이탈리아어, 베트남어, 체코어, 인도네시아어 등으로 번역 출간되었다. 스님은 2012년 5월 22일 0시, 세납 86세로 입적하셨으며, 법랍 63세셨다.

and much, much more. Yet, even when she provided material support, always there was the deep, unseen aid she offered through this connection we all share.

However, she saw that ultimately, for people to live freely and go forward in the world as a blessing to all around them, they needed to know about this bright essence that is within each of us. To help people discover this for themselves, she founded the first *Hanmaum*[4] Seon Center in 1972. For the next forty years she gave wisdom to those who needed wisdom, food and money to those who were poor and hungry, and compassion to those who were hurting.

---

4. Hanmaum[han-ma-um]: "Han" means one, great, and combined, while "maum" means mind, as well as heart, and together they mean everything combined and connected as one.

What is called Hanmaum is intangible, unseen, and transcends time and space. It has no beginning or end, and is sometimes called our fundamental mind. It also means the mind of all beings and everything in the universe connected and working together as one. In English, we usually translate this as "one mind."

본 저서는 대행큰스님의 법문을 한국어와 영어 합본 시리즈로 출간하는 〈생활 속의 참선수행〉 시리즈 제20권으로, 1989년 4월 16일 정기법회 때 설하신 법문에 1994년 10월 23일 전국 청년 연합 법회 때 행해진 질의응답 부분을 첨부하여 재편집하였습니다.

This is volume 20 in the ongoing series, *Practice in Daily Life*, published as a bilingual Korean–English edition of Dharma talks by Daehaeng Kun Sunim.

This edition is a combination of the regular Dharma talk on April 16, 1989, together with the question-and-answer session from the National Youth Association gathering held on October 23, 1994.

Daehaeng Kun Sunim founded nine overseas branches of Hanmaum Seon Center, and her teachings have been translated into twelve different languages to date: English, German, Russian, Chinese, French, Spanish, Indonesian, Italian, Japanese, Vietnamese, Estonian, and Czech, in addition to the original Korean.

For more information about these or the overseas centers, please see the back of this book.

생활 속의 참선수행 시리즈 20

겁내지 않고 당당하게

The Secret To Living Without Fear

겁내지 않고 당당하게

여러분들과 더불어 또 이렇게 한자리를 하게 됐습니다. 여러분들은 이 법당 안에 있는 분들하고만 같이 하는 게 아니라, 우주 만물과도 더불어 한자리를 하고 있는 겁니다.

우리는 전체가 같이 이렇게 한자리를 하고 있고, 그래서 내가 항상 얘기하지만, 우리의 삶이라는 게 공식共食, 공체共體, 공생共生, 공용共用이라는 걸 아셔야 합니다. 거기에 독불장군은 없어요. 그러니 이름을 가지고 이 종교, 저 종교 따지면서 가르지 마십시오. 종교라는 자체가 바로 생활인 것입니다. 종교라는 게 따로 떨어져 있으면 그건 종교가 아니고 부처님이 가르쳐 주신 뜻이 아닙니다.

The Secret to Living Without Fear

We've all come together here once more. We're here together in this Dharma Hall, but it's not just us who are here. Every being, every life, and every form of energy throughout the universe is also here with us.

We all inherently exist together as part of one whole. This is why I'm always telling you that you need to truly understand that we share the same body and life, that we inherently work together as one, freely giving and receiving whatever is needed. This is our fundamental state. There is no single part that exists separate

이러한 가르침을 공부하고자 지금 여기에 여러분들이 모이신 겁니다. 그러니 여러분들이 없다면 부처라는 이름도 없을 거고, 부처라는 이름이 없다면, 부처라는 그 길을 따라서 인간의 도리를 배울 수도 없겠지요. 이렇게 공부하고자 하는 마음이 있기 때문에 참자기를 만나신 분들도 상당히 있을 거라 봅니다.

from everything else. So don't get caught up in dividing religions by names or appearances. True religion is not something apart from life, it is life itself. If religion stands apart from the living, breathing essence of our shared existence, then it is no longer the path that the Buddha pointed towards.

You've gathered here today with the sincere desire to study and live these teachings. And truly, if not for people like you, then the Buddha would not have appeared in this world. And without him, we would not have this path by which people can learn what it means to live as true human beings. It's this sincere aspiration to seek the truth that has led many of you to already come face-to-face with your true nature.

그런데 죽은 영령들이나 산 사람들, 유체有體·무체無體이 모두가 차원이 높고 낮은 이런 문제들과 연결되어 돌아가고 있기 때문에, 여러분들은 여러분들한테 발생하는 일들이 어디서 온 줄도 모르고, 그 고苦에서 헤어나지 못하고 겪어야 할 때가 많을 겁니다. 사실, 보지도 못하고 알지도 못하니 어디서 이런 고통이 왔는지도 모르는 여러분들에게 길을 인도하면서 어떤 때는 참으로 답답한 생각이 들기도 합니다. 하지만 그걸 답답하게 생각해서도 안 되겠죠. 왜냐하면 여러분들은 내가 몰랐을 때의 내 모습이니까요.

Both the living and the dead – those with form and those without – are all intertwined in an intricate web of causes and effects and different levels of consciousness. People don't see this, so they frequently do things that result in hardships and suffering that they don't understand. They don't know why those came to them or how best to respond, and so they end up just suffering and enduring them.

As I witness this, sometimes my heart grows heavy with sorrow. But even so, I know that I shouldn't let myself get frustrated, because that's exactly what I was like when I didn't know any better.

It isn't like I always knew these things. But now that I do, it weighs on me whenever I see someone trapped in their pain, unable to break free. What each of you experiences is not yours alone – it is caught up in the lives and karma of

내가 언제 적부터 알았겠습니까마는, 알고 난 지금에 당해서는 고통에서 헤어 나오지 못하는 여러분들을 볼 때마다 마음이 많이 무겁고 안타깝습니다. 여러분들이 겪는 일들은 여러분 자신 하나만 결부된 게 아니라, 죽은 사람, 산 사람들이 그렇게 다 결부되어 있고, 태胎로 낳는 거, 알로 낳는 거, 또 화化해서 낳는 거, 습濕해서 낳는 거, 이 모든 것이 한데 합쳐져 덩어리가 돼 가지곤 항상 돌아가니까 여러분들은 어디서 연유된지도 모르면서 겪게 되는 그 고통을 면할 길이 없는 겁니다.

되풀이하는 말 같지만, 내가 열 마디 백 마디 같은 말을 하더라도, 침착하게 잘 들으셔서 그것을 지혜롭게 응용하신다면, 여러분이 살아가면서 겪는 고통이 삼분의 일로 줄어들고, 나중에는 그마저도 또 줄어들지 않을까? 이렇게 봅니다.

both the living and the dead. Whether beings are born from the womb, from eggs, through transformation, or from moisture, all are connected together in a vast flow of cause and effect. These karmic strands ceaselessly gather, tangle, and fall apart, forming great knots of pain and confusion. And so, people suffer, unable to know where it all began, struggling to find a way past it.

Even though I repeat myself ten times or a hundred times, listen with a centered mind. If you're able to wisely apply what you hear, the suffering you face in life could be reduced by as much as two thirds. If you keep working diligently at this, then later, even that remaining part may begin to dissolve.

괴로움은
어디에서 오는가?

그렇다면 우선 여러분들은 보지도 못하고 알지도 못하고, 어디서 온 줄도 모르고 어디로 가는 줄도 모르는 이 '고苦' 덩어리 자체가 어디에서 온 거냐? 지난번에도 얘기했듯이 여러분들은 어머니, 아버지에게 살과 뼈를 빌어서 집을 짓고 나왔습니다. 그런데 묘한 것은 여러분들이 그냥 나온 게 아니라 이 세상에 나오기 이전에 한 것들이 딱 그대로 기록된 문서를 짊어지고 나온 겁니다. 이 세상에 나올 때 부모의 힘을 빌어 집만 받아가지고, 그 안에 있는 의식 자체의 덩어리, 고苦 덩어리는 자기가 한 것대로 짊어지고 나온 겁니다.

The role of karmic states of consciousness in suffering

So where does this suffering come from? As I've said before, you were born into this world with the flesh and bones of your mother and father. But in addition to this, you also came carrying a hidden record, a karmic record that was already written before you arrived. These are the *karmic states of consciousness*[5] of everything you have done in the past – each action, word, and intention have gathered and taken form within you. It's this recording, this karmic imprint that is the true weight you carry.

---

5. **Karmic consciousnesses(業識)**: Our thoughts, feelings, and behaviors are recorded as the consciousnesses of the lives that make up our body. These are sometimes called karmic consciousnesses, although they don't have independent awareness or volition. Sometime afterwards, these consciousnesses will come back out. Thus, we may feel happy, sad, angry, etc., without an obvious reason, or they may cause other problems to occur. The way to dissolve these consciousnesses is not to react to them when they arise, and instead to entrust them to our foundation. However, even these consciousnesses are just temporary combinations, so we shouldn't cling to the concept of them.

그런데 짊어지고 나온 것이 내가 어떻게 할 수 없는 종문서 같으면 모르겠는데, 그게 아닌데도 그 문서에 움쭉을 못 하니, 짊어지고 나온 것이 종문서와 매한가지이다 이겁니다. 자기가 바꾸려면 얼마든지 바꿀 수 있는 것을 스스로를 그 문서에 옭아매고 종노릇을 하며 고통을 받는다 이겁니다.

과거 수억 겁 동안 수많은 생을 거치면서 쌓인 **업식** 業識[2]들이 그 고苦 덩어리를 만든 거고, 그래서 그 업식들이 수시로 인연 따라 차례차례 들썩거리며 나고 들면서 자기를 괴롭히는데, 그 고통은 때때로 말로 형용할 수 없을 만큼 괴롭습니다. 자기를 괴롭히기 위해서 식구들을 괴롭히고, 식구들을 괴롭히기 위해서 자기를 괴롭히는데, 보이지 않는 데와 보이는 데가 수없이 연결돼서 돌아가니 그걸 알 길 없는 여러분들은 너무도 기가 막힐 일입니다.

---

2. 업식(業識): 과거 생에 지은 모든 행위와 생각이 현재 우리의 몸속에 있는 생명들의 의식에 그대로 기록되어 잠재되어 있는 것. 때가 되면 이 의식들이 하나씩 풀려나와 여러 가지 형태로 우리들 앞에 펼쳐지게 됨. 이러한 의식들을 녹이는 방법은 발생하는 모든 문제를 자신의 근본 자리에 지속적으로 맡기는 것이며, 업식도 원래는 공(空)한 것이니, 업식이 있다는 생각 자체에 착을 두지 않아야 함.

Now, if that karmic document were something untouchable, then there might be nothing to do but accept it. But it's not like that. The fact is, it can be changed. It can be rewritten. And yet most people live as if it were carved in stone. They're enslaved by their own minds. Though the key is in their own hands, they remain chained to a suffering that no longer has to define them.

Over countless eons and lifetimes, you have accumulated layers upon layers of karmic consciousnesses. Stirred by passing conditions, these karmic recordings rise one after another, disturbing your peace and tormenting you from within and without. Sometimes, the pain is beyond anything words can express. In that pain, you hurt your family in order to hurt yourself, and hurt yourself in order to hurt your family. The visible and invisible are tightly

뼈를 빌고 살을 빌어서 내 집을 짓고는 나왔으나, 종문서 같은 업식을 짊어지고 나왔으니 옴패부득할 수 없이, 거기서 들락날락하는 업식을 어쩌지 못합니다. 그 업식들은 바깥으로는 악의 세균을 끌어들이고 안에서는 반란을 일으키며 병고를 일으키고, 가난을 일으키고, 괴로움, 외로움, 허무감을 일으키니 수 없는 그 나날들이 하루도 편하지 않습니다. 즐거운 거는 잠시 잠깐이고 그저 걱정, 근심 이런 것만이 주어져 있습니다. 젊으면 젊은 대로, 늙으면 늙은 대로, 여자는 여자대로, 남자는 남자대로, 애는 애대로 말입니다.

bound together, interacting and functioning outside your awareness. And so, not knowing what is causing your behavior, or where it comes from, you are left stunned and overwhelmed as one hardship after another continues to arise.

You came into this world by borrowing flesh and bones to build your body, and carried with you the karmic states of consciousness of all you have done. But this record is not truly unchangeable.

Nonetheless, most people live as if they were powerless to alter it, just reacting to these karmic recordings. From the outside, these karmic states of consciousness draw in harmful things, and on the inside, they stir up revolt. Illnesses arise. Poverty takes hold. Sorrow, loneliness, and emptiness grow. Each day becomes a struggle with no peace in sight. Moments of joy are fleeting, while worry and fear settle in like

내가 이런 얘기를 반복해서 일러드리는 건 보이는 것, 보이지 않는 것뿐만 아니라 차원을 넘어 모든 게 같이 얽혀 돌아가기 때문입니다. 그러니까 당연히 우리의 생활, 현재 안팎으로 일어나는 모든 것들, 업식 이런 것들은 따로 떨어져 있는 게 아닙니다. 그런데 여러 번 같은 얘기를 들어도 많은 분들이 진정으로 가슴에 와닿지 않는가 봅니다. 한마디라도 그것을 가슴으로 이해한 사람은 뭔가 달라지는 걸 느낄 수밖에 없는데 "나는 믿는데도 그것이 안 됩니다."라고 합니다.

familiar guests. Whether young or old, woman or man, child or adult, everyone carries their own burden. None are exempt.

I keep telling you about this because everything is functioning as one utterly interconnected whole. All of our daily life, our suffering, everything inside and outside, and all of these karmic states of consciousness are one dynamic whole, where all of it is present here, flowing, and with nothing existing apart from us. Yet even after hearing these teachings repeatedly, there are still many people who don't realize the implications of what I'm saying.

If even just one phrase is really felt and understood, something within will inevitably begin to change. Nonetheless, there are still people who say, "I believe what you're saying, but the problems in my life just don't seem to be improving."

그런데 보세요. 내가 거짓을 얘기하는 게 아닙니다. 전자의 역대 조사祖師들이나 부처님이나, 나나 허투루 말하는 게 아니에요. 그러니까 이 공부를 어영부영하지 마세요. 하려면 제대로 하고 그렇게 하지 않으려면 하지 마세요. 석가모니 부처님께서는 몸을 갈아 재가 되어도 그 재조차 남지 않을 정도로 온 **마음**[3]을 담아서 했기 때문에 모든 것을 걸림 없이 하실 수 있었던 거고, 그렇기에 지금까지도 그 가르침이 여러분들과 더불어 같이 살아 있는 겁니다.

그리고 지금 내가 여러분들한테 길잡이 노릇을 하고 있지만, 무엇보다도 여러분들의 근본마음, **주인공**主人空[4]

---

3. **마음**(心): 단순히 두뇌를 통한 정신활동이나 지성을 일컫는 말이 아니라, 만물만생이 지니고 있으며, 일체 만법을 움직이게 하는 천지의 근본을 뜻함. '안에 있다, 밖에 있다.' 혹은, '이거다 저거다'라고 말할 수 없으며 시작과 끝이 없고 사라질 수도, 파괴될 수도 없음. 시공을 초월하여 존재함.

4. **주인공**(主人空): 우리 모두 스스로 갖추어 가지고 있는 근본마음으로 일체 만물만생의 근본과 직결된 자리. 나를 존재하게 하고, 나를 움직이게 하며, 내 모든 것을 관장하는 참 주인이므로 주인(主人)이며, 매 순간 쉴 사이 없이 변하고 돌아가 고정된 실체가 없으므로 빌 공(空)자를 써서, 주인공(主人空)이라 함.

But let me say this clearly: Not a single word of what I'm saying is untrue. So please, believe this. The buddhas, the patriarchs, and I do not speak lightly. When the Buddha said something could be done, it could be done. So if you want to know for yourself this flowing whole that encompasses everything, then make the effort to do it to the very best of your ability.

When the Buddha practiced, he gave himself wholly to the path, even if it meant wearing down his body to dust, and then continuing until not even the dust remained. That's why he was able to manifest freely, wherever help was needed, and why his teachings remain vibrant and alive today.

Though I may be acting as a guide to you, the real guiding force lies not in me, but within

이 여러분들을 형성하고 이 세상에 나오게 했다는 겁니다. 이러한 나의 근본마음은 내가 지금 살아가고 있는 현실의 생활에 직결되어 있고, 그건 부정할 수 없는 일입니다.

만물만생은 세상에 태어나 살다 죽고, 죽으면 다시 태어나 삽니다. 예전에도 얘기했지만, 생명의 근본은 영원하기 때문에 죽을 게 없어요. 단지 부모에게서 받은 이 몸뚱이는 나를 이루는 자생 중생들의 집과 같고, 밥해 먹는 솥이나 음식을 내놓는 오븐과 같아서 망가지고 부서지면 새걸로 바꿀 뿐입니다. 여러분들이 물건을 사다가 간수를 잘해서 잘 쓰면 조금 오래가는 거고, 간수를 못해서 빨리 망가지면 얼른 갈아야 하는 것과 같아요. 그러니 온전히 나만의 것이라고 할 수도 없는 이 몸을 잘 쓰다 가면 좋겠죠?

you. It is your *Juingong*[6] – your inherent, true self – that formed you and brought you into this world, and is there in everything you experience in your day-to-day life.

All beings and all things are born into this world, live for a time, die, and then are born and live another life. As I've said before, the essence of life is eternal; there is no such thing as death in the ultimate sense. This body you've received from your parents is not who you truly are. It is merely a house, a collection of countless life-forms that work together to sustain you. The body is like a pot in which rice is cooked, or an oven where meals are prepared – when it breaks or wears out, you simply exchange it for a new one. If you care for it well, it lasts a while longer; if you don't, it needs to be replaced sooner.

---

6. Juingong(主人空, [Ju-in-gong]): Pronounced "ju-in-gong." Juin (主人) means the true doer or the master, and gong(空) means empty. Thus, Juingong is our true nature, our true essence, the master within that is always changing and manifesting, with no fixed form or shape.

자기를 해쳐 가며 막 사는 자식들한테 부모가 뭐라고 하면 "그런 건 왜 참견을 합니까?" 이러거든요. 상관하지 말라는 거죠. 부모에게 받은 몸이니 그 몸을 잘 간수하면서 살면 자기만 좋은 게 아니라 효도도 할 수 있는 거거든요. 그런데 효도심 뿐만 아니라 충성심이 깊은 사람들은 부처님 법도 따를 수 있는 그런 지혜로운 착한 마음이 있습니다.

대부분 자식들은 부모가 오래 살길 바라고, 또 부모는 자식이 나보다 빨리 죽으면 안 된다고 생각합니다. 그리고 그렇게 되지 않았을 때 고통을 받게 되죠. 그리고 또 한편으론 죽을 때가 되면 차라리 얼른 죽으면 좋겠는데, 그것도 그렇게 생각처럼 되질 않으니 고통스러워요.

When children harm themselves through reckless living, and their parents try to intervene, they often respond with, "Why are you interfering in my life?" But this body isn't fully "mine," and should be used with care and respect. In fact, caring for your body is, in itself, an act of kindness to your parents.

By the way, there's something that applies to not only the people who care for their parents, but also those people who protect and care for their country. They are both creating good roots that will enable them to put the Buddha's teachings into practice.

People always hope that their parents will live a long time and that their children will not die before them, don't they? But when it doesn't happen that way, it can be unbelievably painful. Likewise, it would be nice if everyone could just leave their body easily when the time comes, but

때로는 부모가 이런저런 욕심이 발단돼서 재산을 다 없애고, 가정을 풍비박산 만들어 온 가족이 가난에 시달리고, 돈이 없으니 작은 병이 생겼을 때 제때 고치지 못해, 큰 병을 만들어 결국 병고에 휘달리게 됩니다. 과거의 업식으로 인해 벌어지는 일들 자체도 버거울 텐데, '이렇게 되면 안 된다. 꼭 저렇게 해야 된다.' 하는 고정된 생각 때문에 또 고통을 받게 되는 거죠.

관觀[5]하는 법을 알아야

언젠가 한 번은 어느 분이 찾아와서 이런 말을 하더라고요. "제가 아파서 병원엘 갔더니 폐암이라고 합니다. 이것을 어떻게 했으면 되겠습니까? 살려주십시오. 아직 출가도 못 시킨 자식이 육 남매나 됩니다.

---

5. 관(觀): 어의적으로 '관찰하다' '보다'라는 뜻을 가지고 있으며, 마음공부를 하는 과정에서는 '참나'인 주인공을 믿고 맡기는 것을 뜻함. 즉, 삶에서 부딪치는 모든 문제들을 주인공만이 해결할 수 있다는 철저한 믿음으로 주인공에게 맡겨 놓고 분별이 없이 집착 없이 지켜보는 것을 통틀어 '관'이라 함.

unfortunately, sometimes people's suffering drags on for years. They spend their money on more and more desperate treatments until nothing is left. Then their family ends up with no money to treat other minor problems, and those sometimes lead to even more serious medical issues. So the family suffers even more. Our karmic states of consciousness cause one sort of problem when they arise, but our fixed ideas about how to respond often add an extra layer of suffering.

Learn how to dissolve karmic states of consciousness before you have need

One day, a man came to see me and said, "I went to the hospital because I wasn't feeling well, and they told me I have lung cancer. What should I do? Please help me. I have six children who still live at home and need me. I lost my mother when

저는 두 살 때 어머니를 잃고 아버지가 새 장가를 들었는데, 새어머니가 너무 구박해서 외할머니 집에서 자랐습니다. 그런데 외할머니도 제가 스무 살이 되기도 전에 돌아가셔서 외숙모 손에서 자랐는데, 무지한 고통과 아픔을 겪게 되어 수차례 죽으려고도 했지만 죽지 못했습니다. 그렇게 고생을 하며 살다 이제 겨우 집이라도 한 칸 장만해서 살만하니까 이런 병이 들었습니다. 제가 못나서 자식들을 제대로 기르질 못했고, 아내도 여태 고생만 시켰는데 이제는 어떻게 해야 좋을지 모르겠습니다." 이렇게 말하면서 눈을 꿈벅거리지도 않았는데 눈물을 줄줄 흘리는 거예요. 그 모습을 보니 마치 전자의 내가 그 사람의 부모였는데 일찍 죽어 두고 온 내 자식을 다시 본 것 마냥, 얼마나 딱하고 불쌍했는지 모릅니다.

I was just two, and my father remarried. But my stepmother was terribly cruel, so I was raised by my maternal grandmother. She too passed away when I was young, and after that, I lived with my aunt and uncle, where I went through so much pain and suffering. There were times I wanted to end my life, but I couldn't. Somehow, I made it through those years. I even managed to buy a little house, and things were finally starting to settle down..., and now I've been struck with this illness. We never had money for anything special or tutoring for the children, and my wife has suffered so much because of my low income. I just don't know what to do."

As he spoke, tears streamed down his face. As I looked at him, it felt as if I had been his parent in a previous life, and now was seeing my child once more. My heart ached with sorrow and helplessness.

너무 불쌍해서 그 순간에 그 집엘 떠억 가보니 할아버지, 할머니, 삼촌, 고모 이런 사람들이 전부 타버린 채로 있더란 말입니다. 6.25 전쟁 때 방안에 잔뜩 가둬 놓고 누가 불을 질러 전부 타버린 겁니다. 그런데 자기 갈 길을 가지 못한 영령들이 여전히 불에 타고 있는 형상으로 비슬비슬하면서 고통받는 의식들을 그대로 가진 채 그 집 방에 잔뜩 있더라고요. 끔찍해서 안보는 게 낫기도 하겠지만, 이런 일들을 아무것도 알지 못하는 후손들은 얼마나 괴로움을 당하며 살았겠습니까? 물론 선조 대로서 자손들을 잘못되게 하려는 건 아니지만 그들이 얼마나 괴로우면 집 안에서 그러고들 있겠습니까? 도움은 필요한데, 어디 가지는 못하고 인연이 그렇게 되어 있으니까, 피붙이라는 의식이 있으니 거기 그렇게 와 있을 수밖에는 없는 거죠.

Feeling the depths of such suffering, in that moment, I wanted to see how he was living, so, through *mind*,[7] I visited his home. And there, I saw them – his grandfather, grandmother, uncles, aunts – all with horrible burns, trying to reach out to the man.

During the Korean War, they had been locked in a room, and someone set fire to the house. They died in the flames. But their spirits had not moved forward. They were still as they were in that room – maimed, smoldering, and writhing in pain from the fire. Things like this are so horrible that most people are better off not knowing about them.

But imagine being one of their descendants, living unaware of the problem, yet constantly

---

7. Mind(心) (Kor. –maum): In Mahayana Buddhism, "mind" refers to this fundamental mind, and almost never means the brain or intellect. It is intangible, beyond space and time, and has no beginning or end. It is the source of everything, and everyone is endowed with it.

그런데 죽은 그 아버지는 아들을 위해서 뭐 좀 도와주고 싶어도 할 수 있는 게 없어요. 아버지가 전자에 해 놓은 게 없다 보니 아들을 살릴 도리가 없단 말입니다. 그래서 그런 조상들은 열 분이 있고 백 분이 있다 해도 여러분들을 도와줄 수가 없어요. 그래서 항상 여러분한테 가르쳐 주는 거예요. 내 근본인 주인공만이 해결할 수 있다는 믿음을 가지고 거기에 다 맡기시라고요. 그래야 나 자신도 돕고 그것이 **공덕**[6]이 되어 자손들도 도울 수 있는 겁니다.

---

6. 공덕(功德): 이 책에서의 의미는 다른 사람이나 대상을 나와 둘로 보지 않고 '내가 했다.'라는 생각을 하지 않으며 조건 없이 도와주는 상태, 혹은 그렇게 함으로써 나오는 결과를 뜻한다. '함이 없이 하는 것' 즉, '내가 이러이러한 일을 했다.'라는 생각을 놓아버리고 해야 공덕이 됨. 아무런 조건 없이 하는 행(行)이라야만 만물만생에게 이익이 될 수 있음.

experiencing inexplicable suffering. It's not that the relatives wanted to harm him or his children, it's just that their torment was so terrible that, in their pain, they were reaching out across the bonds of *karmic affinity,*[8] desperate for help and solace. And who has greater karmic affinity than family?

But even the spirit of his father, who had by then also passed away, could do nothing. He had not practiced spiritual cultivation during his lifetime, nor had he done much to help others, so there just wasn't any path open to him that would enable him to help his son. Even though you have a hundred ancestors wanting to help, they cannot unless they've laid some kind of a foundation.

That is why I keep telling you: Only your Juingong, your true self, has the power to resolve

---

8. Karmic affinity(因緣): The connection or attraction between people or things due to previous karmic relationships.

여러분, 이 물그릇에다가 물 열 방울을 갖다가 넣으면 이게 두드러집니까? 그냥 한 그릇의 물이죠? 방 안에 있던 그 조상님들을 이 그릇에다 전부 넣으시면 한 그릇의 물이 됩니다. 이해가 가시나요? 다행히도 힘들어하던 그분은 내 말을 잘 이해해서, 방안은 깨끗해지고 용기를 얻게 됐습니다. 그분은 지금도 강원도 어딘가에서 잘 살고 있습니다.

such karmic entanglements. Entrust everything to this root within you. When you do, not only can you help yourself, but that also becomes a blessing that can support your children and their children in unimaginable ways.

Now imagine this: if you put ten drops of water into a cup of water, do those drops remain separate? No, they simply become one with the water already there. In the same way, when you gather those troubled spirits and bring them into the oneness of your foundation, they too will be absorbed into that great stillness and clarity. Do you understand what this means? Fortunately, the man who had been suffering truly understood what I was saying. And once he entrusted everything to his Juingong, all the suffering in that room vanished, and he found renewed courage. He's now living a pleasant life somewhere in Gangwon Province.

사실, 인간이라면, 살고 죽고를 떠나서, 인간으로서 받은 은혜를 알고, 진정한 사랑을 알아야 합니다. 그러면 조상과 부처가 둘이 아니라는 그 뜻을 알 겁니다. 부처도 조상이요, 조상도 부처다 이런 소리가 있죠? 이 뜻은 뭐냐면 모두가 자기요, 자식이요, 내 부모란 뜻입니다. 내 물 한 그릇에다 다 집어넣어도 두드러지지 않는, 줄지도 늘지도 않는 묘법을 말하는 거지요. 그러니 모든 걸 내 안에 다 놓는다면 부처님의 속도 뚫어지게 알 수 있겠죠. 그런데 만약 여러분이 하나하나 내 안에 놓고 가며 알게 되는 체험을 하지 못한다면, 깨달아 가는 것도 없고, 그러니 자신을 승화시키지도 못하며, 결국 둘 아니게 나투며 돌아가는 이치도 모르게 됩니다.

In truth, regardless of what your life is like, if you realize the full extent of the grace and love that you've received by being born and living as a human being, you will truly understand what it means when someone says, "Buddhas and ancestors are not two." It means that everyone is myself, everyone is my child and my parent.

This reality of nonduality means that no matter what you put into this cup of water, it won't overflow. And no matter how much you use, it won't shrink. Everything fits without the least disturbance. It's so amazing and profound. When you entrust everything inwardly, you will come to thoroughly understand Buddha as well.

But if you don't have the deep experiences that come from entrusting inwardly what you're going through and then moving forward, no true awakening can occur. No transformation of

맡겨 놓고
빙긋이 웃을 수 있는

우리 이 부장도 갑자기 엉덩이가 삐뚤어져서, 허리가 아프고 걷기도 힘들어지니 별짓 다 했어요. 여러 사람들이 병원에 가서 엑스레이 섯건 검사를 모두 받아보라고 했대요. 그러면서 날 보고 병원에 간다고 그러더라고요.

your awareness or *habits*[9] will happen, and you won't perceive the nondual arising and interacting of all things.

Sometimes, what you're going through is your true self testing you

Mr. Lee, who works for the *Seon*[10] Center, hurt his back so badly that he could barely even walk. He tried everything he could think of, and people around him kept telling him to go to the hospital and get X-rays taken and such. One day, he mentioned this to me, saying that he thought he needed to go to the hospital.

---

9. habits(習): These include not just the ways of thought and behavior learned in this life, but also all of those tendencies of thought and behavior that have accumulated over endless eons.

10. Seon(禪) (Chan, Zen): Seon describes the unshakeable state where one has firm faith in their inherent foundation, their Buddha-nature, and so returns everything they encounter back to this funda-mental mind. It also means letting go of "I," "me," and "mine" throughout one's daily life.

그래서 내가 그랬습니다. "네가 어려서부터 입산을 해서 행자 노릇을 하고, 중노릇을 하다 군대를 갔는데 그리곤 그만 속퇴를 했다. 그렇더라도 네가 그냥 갈 수는 없지 않느냐? 너는 지금 병에 걸린 게 아니다. 너를 테스트하는 중이야. 내가 이렇게 얘기해주는데도 네가 그걸 안으로 놓아가며 수행을 하지 않고, 바깥으로 그렇게 떠돌면 너는 언제 너를 발견하겠느냐!" 그런데도 무슨 큰 병에 걸린 게 아닌가 걱정을 하면서 이것저것 검사를 받아야겠다 하더라구요. 주위의 사람들을 위해서라도 그렇게 해야겠다 하면서요. 그런데 병원에서는 척추가 좀 휜 거 외에는 깨끗하고 별다른 이상이 없다고 그랬대요.

After looking deep within him, I said, "You entered the mountains and trained as a novice monk from a young age. You lived as a monk but later went into the army, and afterward, you left the path and returned to secular life.

"Even so, do you really think you can just go on through life without facing your true self? This isn't a disease – you're being tested. Even though I'm telling you what this pain really is, if you don't reflect deeply on these words and work on putting their implications into practice, and instead keep wandering around, focused outwardly, when will you ever come to know who you truly are?"

But still, he kept worrying, wondering if he might have some serious illness, and he also wanted to get tested for the peace of mind of those around him. In the end, the doctors told him that apart from a slight curvature of the

부처님 법은 묘하고 광대무변합니다. 그러니 여러분들이 아플 때 그걸 병이라고만 생각하지 말고, 내가 공부할 수 있는 기회이기도 함을 아시고, 모든 걸 내 근본에 자꾸 놓으세요. 그러면 진짜 큰 병에 걸렸더라도 겁이 안 납니다. 지금 죽는다 하더라도 만물만생과 하나로 돌아가는 내 근본을 철저하게 믿으세요. 그럼 겁날 게 없습니다. 뭐, 그렇게 걱정을 하세요. 여기 여러분들에게 어떤 병이 있다 할지라도 여러분의 한생각[7]이 중요합니다. 자기 근본을 믿는 그 한생각이 자기를 구덩이에서 벗어나게 할 수 있는 묘법이거든요.

---

7. 한생각: 어떤 생각을 우리들 내면의 근본 자리에 입력시키거나 맡겨 놓았을 때, 근본을 통해 나오는 생각은 우리들 몸속의 모든 생명들뿐만 아니라 이 세상의 만물만생에 전달되며, 일체가 그 생각에 응하게 됨. 보이지 않는 정신계, 즉 우리들 근본마음을 통해 일으켜지는 생각은 물질계에서 현실로 나타나게 됨. 이렇게 근본을 통해 나오게 되는 생각을 한생각이라 함.

spine, everything was fine and there was nothing wrong.

The potential of these teachings is so profound and beyond anything you can imagine. So, when you're sick, don't just see that as an illness. Recognize it as an opportunity to deepen your practice, and keep placing everything into your *fundamental mind*.[11] Then, even if you are facing a serious illness, you won't be afraid. Even if you were about to die right now, hold fast to the deep trust that your true foundation is functioning as one with all beings and all things. Then, there's nothing to fear. Why worry so much?

---

11. Fundamental mind: This refers to our inherent essence, that which we fundamentally are. "Mind," in Mahayana Buddhism, almost never means the brain or intellect. Instead, it refers to the essence, through which we are connected to everything, everywhere. It is intangible, beyond space and time, and has no beginning or end. It is the source of everything, and everyone is endowed with it. "Fundamental mind" is interchangeable with other terms such as "Buddha-nature," "true nature," "true self," and "foundation."

여러분들은 여러분들 스스로 창살 없는 감옥에다가 옹쳐매놓고 있습니다. 어디가 아프면 병자로 옹쳐매놓고 있고, 가난하면 가난한 대로, 돈이 많으면 많은 대로, 자기를 옭아매고 가둡니다. 그러니 더 고통스러울 수밖에 없지요. 모든 건 여러분들의 생각에 달려 있습니다. 과거의 자기가 한 대로 그대로 문서를 가지고 나와 그 모진 고통을 받는다 하더라도, 자기 근본을 믿고 거기에 다 맡기는 한생각에, 그 고통과 그 종문서를 한꺼번에 태워 버릴 수 있습니다. 자꾸 놓다 보면 스스로 되게 돼 있단 말입니다.

Even if you are facing some illness, what truly matters is connecting with your foundation. For, entrusting a thought there, to your foundation, is a truly profound and mysterious thing that can lift you out of any pit.

You are the ones who have locked yourselves inside a prison that has no walls or bars. When your body aches, you trap yourself in the identity of a sick person. When you're poor, you bind yourself with the idea of poverty. And even when you're wealthy, you still imprison yourself in that wealth. No wonder suffering continues. Everything depends on your own thoughts.

Even if you face suffering that arises from the karmic records you've carried into this life, just *one thought*[12] of trusting your foundation

---

12. One Thought: This refers to the ability to raise and then input and entrust a thought to our foundation. When we can connect with our foundation like this, then through our foundation, that thought spreads to everything in the universe, including all of the lives in our body. At that instant, because all things are fundamentally not two, they all respond to that thought.

전에도 얘기했지만, 과거도 없고, 미래도 없고, 현재도 없습니다. 구분 없이 하나로 같이 돌아가는 거예요. 한 찰나刹那 살림살이일 뿐입니다. 그리고 우리의 살림살이는 한 찰나의 나툼일 뿐이고요, 그 한 찰나의 살림살이가 그렇게 요리 변덕, 조리 변덕 하면서, 도깨비장난 같고, 귀신장난감 같거든요. 그걸 말로 하려니까 이렇게밖에 표현을 못 하겠는데, 여하간에 여러분들 자체를 포함해서 가만히 있는 게 하나도 없어요. 계속 움직이고 변하고 그래요. 변화무쌍합니다.

and entrusting everything to it can burn away both that suffering and those karmic records all at once. If you keep letting go of everything you encounter, again and again, you'll notice that the things you're facing begin to resolve on their own.

As I've said before, there is no past, no future, and no present. There is no true division of time. The past, present, and future all unfold together as one, inseparably. What we call our life is nothing more than a single moment of arising and vanishing. And within that moment everything keeps shifting and changing in unpredictable ways, like a goblin's prank or a ghost's plaything. It's hard to adequately express this in words, but there's not a single thing that remains still, including you yourself. Everything is constantly moving, shifting, and transforming. It's truly beyond anything you can imagine.

여러분들이 아무 생각 없이 공에 들어서 가만히 있다면 그건 목석木石인 거죠. 또 아는 척을 너무 많이 해서 한데 떨어뜨리면 그건 귀신인 거구요. 그러니까 여러분이 안팎으로 무슨 일이 벌어지던 내 근본마음, 주인공만을 믿고 거기에 다 놓으면서 가세요. 여러분이 화가 나면 화가 나는 대로 '화가 나는구나.' 하시면서 거기에도 걸리지 마십시오. 여러 생각이 자꾸 나걸랑 그것도 그냥 그러려니 하세요. 그저 업식이 들고 나면서 괴로움도 주고 즐거움도 주고 이러는 거니까요.

If you meditate and just focus on maintaining a sense of tranquility and peacefulness without any awareness of your foundation, you're no different from a piece of wood or stone. And if you're pretending to know more than you do and leading people astray, you're already a ghost.

So no matter what arises, whether it's inside or outside, stay focused on your fundamental mind, Juingong. Entrust it with all of that and continue forward. When anger arises, just acknowledge it, "Ah, I'm feeling angry." Let it be, but don't get caught in it. When all sorts of thoughts keep surfacing, just accept them as they are. These are only your karmic consciousnesses as they arise and disappear, causing you joy one moment and suffering the next.

But all of it is arising from your Juingong, your fundamental mind, so, just return it there. When you do this, there is nothing for them to latch

그것도 다 내 주인공, 근본마음에서 나온 거니 거기에 그냥 다 놓으세요. 거긴 아무것도 붙지 않습니다. 그러니 자꾸 내가 이렇다 저렇다 하면서 괜히 더 힘들어하지 마시고, 즐겁더라도 괴롭더라도 빙긋이 웃고 마세요. 거기서 밖엔 해결 못 하거든요. '네 속에서 나온 건 네 속에서 해결해. 난 업식에서 나온 이 도깨비장난 같은 것들에 속지 않을 거야. 그게 큰 부처로 내 앞에 보이더래도 난 거기에 속지 않아.' 이런 단단한 마음으로 업식의 나툼에 이리저리 휘둘리지 말고 내 근본마음에 모든 걸 맡기세요.

onto. Don't make things harder by clinging to ideas such as "I like this." Whether you're happy or suffering, just smile gently and let it pass.

Your foundation is the only thing that can truly take care of this stuff. Say to yourself, "The things arising from within can only be solved from within. So no matter how tricky or seductive these karmic consciousnesses are, I won't be fooled by them. Even if they appear before me as a great buddha, I won't be deceived."

Go forward with this kind of firmness, and don't let yourself be pushed around by these karmic manifestations. Leave everything to your true, inherent mind.

To put it another way, you've come into this world carrying the karmic record you created, like a file that you yourself uploaded. But don't be deceived by the things that arise and fall within it.

다시 말하자면 자기가 한 것대로 입력된 문서를 종문서처럼 쥚어지고는 나왔지만 거기서 들고 나는 것들에는 속지 마시라 이겁니다. 누가 "어디 가면 용하다더라. 좋은 말씀 많이 한다." 이러더라도 그런 것에 속지 마세요. 잘 살펴서 말, 뜻, 행, 이 세 가지가 일치하는지 똑바로 보시고, 만약 그러하다면, 그래서 그 사람의 진실한 뜻을 알게 되면 배울 점이 많은 훌륭한 사람으로 따르세요. 나를 포함해서 하는 말입니다. 하지만 믿는 건 오직 내 근본마음이어야 합니다. 왜 그러냐? 주인공 안에는 나와 더불어, 일체 만물만생이 다 같이 한자리를 하고 있기 때문입니다.

내가 한 생각과 말과 행동은
그대로 내게 돌아온다

예전에 한 남자가 타력 신앙이 아닌 자력 신앙으로써, 자기 안으로 모든 걸 놓으면서, 아주 진실하고 청정하게 부처님 공양을 잘했어요. 그래서 자기 손자가 왕이 된 거죠.

Someone might say, "There's a great teacher over there," or "They give wonderful talks." But don't be deceived by such things. Look closely: do their words, intentions, and actions all align? If they do, then there will definitely be things you can learn from them. These standards apply to me as well.

But the one you should truly trust is your own fundamental mind. Why? Because within there, all things abide together as one. You are there, all buddhas are there, and all beings are there, together as one whole.

Everything you give rise to becomes part of yourself

Once, there was a man who, instead of seeking gods or buddhas outside of himself, practiced by seeking inwardly. He entrusted everything

손주를 왕으로 만들려고 노력한 게 아니라 덕을 쌓다 보니 그렇게 된 거예요.

그리고 덕을 많이 쌓았던 그 남자는 자기 손주의 삼대 아래 손자로 태어나 대통령이 되었죠. 그렇게 대통령이 되었으면 그 전보다도 더 자기중심을 잡고 수행을 하며 덕을 쌓아야 하는데, 대통령이 되다 보니 권력이 많아져서 욕심이 커진 겁니다. 욕심이 커지면 눈에 보이는 게 없어지고 옳은 말은 들리지도 않게 되죠. 당연히 맑고 단단했던 자기중심은 흐리멍덩해지면서 남의 소리에 우왕좌왕하게 되고 점점 더 업식의 '고苦 덩어리'가 장난질을 쳐대어 욕심은 더 커지게 된 겁니다.

inwardly, and offered aid to people and religious communities that was pure and free of any selfishness. As a result, his grandson ended up becoming king. He hadn't been trying to make this happen, of course, but he had accumulated so much *virtue and merit*[13] that's what happened.

He was later reborn as the great-grandson of his grandson, and because of his virtue and merit, became president. But now as president, he needed to practice even harder, for, no matter how well he had done in the past, he still needed to be focused on his clear and upright center. Instead, as his power grew, so did his desire. And when desire grows, you lose sight of what's right and become deaf to the voice of truth.

---

13. Virtue and merit(功德): Here this term refers to the results of helping unconditionally and nondually, without any thought of self or other. It becomes virtue and merit when it is "done without doing," that is, done without the thought that "I did." Because it is done unconditionally, all beings benefit from it.

권력을 유지하려고 얼마나 많은 사람들을 핍박하고 또 죽게도 했겠어요. 측근들끼리 작당 모의해가며 아무도 모르게 한다고 했겠지만, 죽임을 당한 그 사람이 알고 그 가족들이 아는데 그 원망이 어디로 가겠습니까? 항상 그 마음이, 의식이 자기를 맴돌고 있단 말입니다. 그렇게 남을 해친 사람은 온전한 생生을 살 수가 없어요. 사람들 눈에 안 보일 뿐이지 그런 의식들이 맴돌기 때문에 산다는 게 그냥 시들거리면서 길을 걷는 거나 마찬가지인 겁니다. 지금도 벌어지는 일이고 과거 수백 년 수천 년 역사에도 허다하게 벌어진 일이에요.

Inevitably, the bright center he once had started to fade. He became swayed by other's voices, unable to stay grounded. The mass of karmic consciousnesses within him began to stir and play their tricks, feeding his desire even more.

Think about how many people he must have oppressed or even had killed in order to maintain his power. He and his inner circle may have worked in secret, thinking no one knew, but the ones who were killed knew. Their family knew. And where do you think that resentment goes?

That consciousness, that energy, constantly circles around the one who caused the harm. All that resentment, their crushed hopes, their dreams cut short settled there, unseen. Do you think such a person experiencing this could then live a whole and peaceful life? Even though it seems like someone got away with their actions,

그래서 마음을 잘 써야 한다는 말을 하는 겁니다. 과거에 덕을 많이 쌓아 지금 안락한 생을 누리는 것처럼 보여도, 여러분의 살림살이는 한 찰나의 나툼일 뿐, 고정된 게 아니에요. 자기 근본에 모든 걸 맡기면서 마음을 잘 쓰고 살면, 만물만생이 근본을 통해 같이 돌아가는 거라 스스로 우주간 법계에서 돌보게 돼 있어요.

those unseen karmic energies continue to circle them, draining them of joy and vitality. Even though they're not dead, they may as well be. People don't think about this because they can't see it, but it's true and has happened time and time again throughout human history.

That's why we say it's so important to use your mind well. Even though the virtue and merit you've created has enabled you to enjoy a comfortable life, this existence is still nothing more than a fleeting manifestation. There's nothing fixed about it. But if you entrust everything to your fundamental mind and live by wisely using this connection to respond to what you face and to help others, then, as all beings and all things move together with you through this same source, the entire universe naturally takes care of you.

아까도 얘기했지만, 병, 가난, 괴로움, 허무감, 이런 것들은 업식의 나툼으로 도깨비장난 같은 거니까 그런 것에 속지 마세요. 그냥 나 테스트하는 거니까 공부하는 계기로 나를 인도하는구나, 감사하다 생각하며 모든 걸 내 주인공, 내 근본마음을 믿고 맡기세요. 정말 쉽지 않겠지만 그렇게 한다면, 이 오장육부 모든 세포의 의식이 **한마음**[8] 한뜻이 되어 **보살**[9]로 화하고, 나의 수호신이 되어 나를 보살필 겁니다. **보현**보살[10], 약사보살이 돼 가지고 보살피니 아픈 다리는 낫는지도 모르게 좋아지고 침침했던 눈도 밝아집니다.

---

8. **한마음**: '한'이란 광대무변함, 일체가 하나로 합쳐진 것을 뜻하며, 한마음이란 만질 수도 없고 보이지도 않으며, 시공간을 초월하여, 시작도 끝도 없는 근본마음을 말함. 또한, 만물만생의 마음이 삼천대천세계와 서로 연결되어 하나로 돌아가는 것을 의미하기도 함. 다시 말해, 한마음은 우주 전체와 그 속에서 살고 있는 일체 생명들이 근본을 통해 서로 연결되어 그 마음들이 하나로 돌아가는 모든 작용을 포함하고 있음.

9. **보살**: 위로는 불법(佛法)을 닦아 깨달음의 지혜를 얻고, 아래로는 중생을 구제하며 그들이 스스로 깨닫도록 도와주는 부처의 화현.

10. **보현**(普賢): 문수보살과 나란히 석가모니불의 보처(補處)로서 이(理), 정(定), 행(行)의 덕(德)을 맡아보는 보살. 흰 코끼리를 타고 있는 모습으로 표현되며 부처님의 우측에서 부처님의 중생 교화, 제도를 보좌하는, 일체 보살의 상수(上首)로 알려져 있음.

As I said earlier, illness, poverty, sorrow, and feelings of meaninglessness are nothing more than those karmic states of consciousness playing tricks on you. So don't get caught up in them. Don't be deceived by them. They're just tests. Don't get stuck on thinking of them in terms of labels such as "disease" or whatever. Instead, remind yourself that, "This suffering is my foundation guiding me forward and giving me opportunities to practice." And then gratefully entrust whatever you're going through.

This won't be easy, but when you do that, the consciousness of every organ and cell in your body will unite as one, and in so doing, they will transform into *bodhisattvas*.[14] They will

---

14. Bodhisattva(菩薩): This usually refers to a person of great spiritual ability who is dedicated to saving those lost in ignorance and suffering. But it also means the applied energy of our fundamental nature, used to help save beings. It can also be described as the non-dual wisdom of enlightenment being used to help others awaken for themselves.

이렇게 내 안의 중생을 나와 둘 아니게 돌아가게끔 할 수 있다면, 여러분들 스스로 자루 없는 자비의 칼이 되어 우주법계를 꿰뚫어서, 죽은 세상 산 세상을 넘나 다니면서 괴롭고, 외롭고, 고독하고, 가난하고, 아픈 사람을 나와 둘 아니게 보듬을 수 있는 그런 여건이 됩니다. 그런 여건이 여러분들 앞에 주어진다는 얘깁니다. 내가 지금 옛날이야기 하는 게 아닙니다. 현재 그렇게 연결돼서 돌아가고 있다는 얘길 하는 거예요.

become your protectors, watching over you like *Samantabhadra*[15] or the Medicine Bodhisattva. Then, without even realizing it, pain and illnesses will fade and become better.

If you can truly become one with the sentient beings within you, working together as one, then you become a sword of compassion, piercing through all of the universes of this vast *Dharma realm*.[16] You will find yourself moving freely between the realms of the living and the dead, able to embrace as one all those who are suffering, lonely, poor, or in pain.

---

15. Samantabhadra(普賢): The bodhisattva who represents the enlightened application of wisdom in the world. Samantabhadra is usually portrayed as riding a white elephant, and helps the Buddha educate and save unenlightened beings. He is often paired with Manjushri.

16. Dharma realm(法界): The level of reality where everything functions as an interpenetrated and connected whole. Daehaeng Kun Sunim said that this can also be called the Dharma Net and compared it to our circulatory system, which connects and nourishes every single cell in the body.

내가 처해 있는 상황을 제대로 보려면

언젠가 어느 분이 이런 얘기를 하더라구요. "스님, 스님이 그렇게 잘 아신다면 왜 지금 노사분규나 학생들이 벌납뛰듯, 미친 듯이 날뛰는데 왜 이걸 그냥 둬서 나라를 위태하게 합니까?" 이러는데 아무것도 모르는 사람한테 내가 무슨 말을 해야 되겠습니까? 내가, 부처님 법은 이러이러하니까 이렇다 한들 그 사람이 이해할 수도 없는데 말이에요.

This isn't some fairytale. This is how it really works.

Deepen your experience so that you can see truly

One day, someone said to me, "*Sunim*,[17] if what you say about the mind and its ability to act upon the world is true, then why do you allow things like labor strikes and student protests to rage on and endanger the country?" But to ask a question like this shows that he didn't have any experience of his fundamental nature. Without this sort of experience, even if I had answered him in detail, telling him about how this realm is truly working, he wouldn't have understood what I was saying.

---

17. Sunim: Sunim is the respectful title of address for a Buddhist monk or nun in Korea.

그래서 이런 말을 했죠. “나쁜 거, 좋은 거, 몽우리 같은 거를 체로 쳐서 골라내려면 모든 국민들이 알아야겠죠. 나쁜 거 좋은 거 전부를 알게 되면 그때는 스스로 체에 쳐집니다.”라고요. 자기가 나쁘면 국민들을 우롱하고 국민들에게 해를 입히게 된 거니 스스로 체에 쳐져서 그냥 밀려 저 땅으로 내버려지게 되어 있어요. 알쭌한 알맹이들은 잘 쓰게 돼 있고 먹을 만한 무거리는 다시 찧어서 먹게끔 된다 이겁니다.

So instead, I just told him, "Before you try to judge who's good and who's bad, you better truly understand everything from top to bottom. If you thoroughly understood all of this, you'd realize that it's all automatically sorting itself out."

If someone is deceiving people, if they're leaving individuals and society worse off, then they will be inevitably, and automatically, sifted out. They'll be tossed aside like useless chaff. Like with rice, the good kernels will be used as they are, and those that are damaged and malformed, but still nutritious, will be milled again and made into something that can be eaten.

When you cook rice porridge, and it starts to boil, it really bubbles and froths, doesn't it? A big bubble bursting here is like one country boiling over, a small bubble popping there is like a disturbance in another country, and even within

죽을 쑤다 보면 펄펄 끓을 때 부글부글하면서 방울방울 올라오지 않습니까? 이 나라에선 이렇게 나오고, 저 나라에선 저렇게 나오고, 한 나라에서도 내가 잘났다, 못났다 하면서 팥죽 끓듯 끓어오릅니다. 그럴 때 주걱 든 사람이 불룩하게 올라오는 건 치고, 안 올라오는 건 올리고 하면서 사방으로 튀지 않게, 뭉치지 않게 잘 저어 맛있게 끓여서 다들 먹을 수 있게끔 하는 거죠. 그냥 주걱이 다 하는 거죠, 뭐. 그렇게 할 수 있는 마음들이 돼야 해요. 그러는 동안 바람이 불어도 그건 상관이 없어요. 그리고 체 치는 건 오히려 바람이 불어야 잘 거를 수 있지 않나 이렇게 봅니다.

a single bubble there are smaller bubbles, each like people shouting, "I'm right!" and "You're wrong!"

Then, the one holding the stirring spoon steps in. They press down on what's swelling too much, lift up what hasn't risen, and stir things evenly, so nothing splatters too much or clumps up. Bit by bit, the porridge cooks evenly and becomes something everyone can share.

You have to practice diligently so that you will be able to take care of the porridge like this. In the course of stirring the porridge, the winds may blow, but that doesn't matter. In fact, when it comes to sifting things out, a good breeze actually helps the process.

Someone once demanded, "How could the Buddha have allowed the very kingdom that gave birth to him to end up being so brutally destroyed?" But that wasn't the Buddha's doing.

예전에 누가 "부처님은 왜 자기가 태어난 데를 저렇게 망가질러 놨을까요?"라고 묻더군요. 근데 그건 부처님이 그런 게 아닙니다. 이 세상을 밥 짓는 솥이라고 한다면 밥을 짓는 사람들이 솥을 망가뜨린 거지요. 망가뜨리지 않고 밥을 잘 지어가며 살면 제일 좋겠지만, 한편으론 솥을 망가뜨려 봐야 솥이 참 필요하구나 하는 걸 절실히 깨닫게 되니 솥을 망가뜨린 게 결과적으로 한 방편의 길잡이가 된다고 볼 수도 있겠습니다. 그래서 생각해 보면 광대무변하고 묘하게 작용하는 이 **권도법**權道法[11]이라는 게 아주 귀중한 보배입니다. 우리나라의 문제도 여러분들이 이 주관만 튼튼히 세워서 가신다면, 다시 말해 자기 근본을 믿고 거기에 일체를 맡겨 놓으면서 가신다면 크게 잘못되는 건 없을 겁니다.

---

11. 권도법(權道法): 사전적 의미는 목적 달성을 위하여 그때그때의 형편에 따라 임기응변으로 일을 처리하는 방도를 말한다. 그러나 큰스님이 말씀해 주신 권도법은 중용으로써 용도에 따라 자유자재할 수 있는 자유자재권을 뜻함. 이는 좋고 나쁜 것이 닥쳐도, 누가 뭐래도 흔들리지 않는, 특히 석존이 와도 흔들리지 않는 그런 사람이라야만 쓸 수 있음.

Look at it this way, a country is like a cooking pot. When it's damaged, it's because people misused it.

Of course, it would be best if they lived wisely and didn't break the pot. But sometimes, it's only after the pot gets broken that people truly realize how essential it was. In that sense, the breaking of the pot might become a means of awakening, something that could be used for guidance along our path.

This story of the Buddha's homeland reminds us of why this vast and profound power that comes from staying centered on our fundamental mind and entrusting it with whatever we face is such a precious treasure. This wisdom and mysterious ability to affect our world is beyond anything we can imagine. Even for problems involving the nation, if you trust your fundamental mind and keep letting go of

이 세상 모든 것은 내 근본마음인 주인공을 통해 하나로 연결되어 고정됨이 없이 찰나찰나 돌아가기 때문에 나의 한생각이 세상을 바꿀 수 있습니다. 그래서 이 세상이 아무리 위대하다 해도, 이 우주의 어떤 것이 위대하다 해도 아주 조그맣고 하찮게 보이는 여러분들의 마음, 그 근본마음보다 더 귀중하고 고귀한 보배는 없을 겁니다. 보이지도 않는 그 조그마한 것이 바로 우주를 삼킬 수도 있으니까 말이에요.

그러니까 인간이 이렇게 위대한 자기 근본을 발견하고, 자기를 승화시키며, 체험하고, 이래서 진정으로 만물만생이 둘이 아님을 깨닫고, 또 둘 아니게 나툼을 깨닫게 된다면 진정한 자유인이 될 것입니다.

everything to it, then things won't go terribly wrong, not in any real or lasting way.

Everything in this world is connected through Juingong, our fundamental mind. There's nothing that remains unchanging. All things ceaselessly flow and change from one instant to the next, so even a single thought is capable of changing the world. No matter how amazing this world may seem, or how untouchable the universe may appear, there is nothing more precious or noble than your own fundamental mind. Though small and invisible, this very mind holds the power to move the entire universe.

We have to discover our own inherent foundation, and then develop our awareness of it through application of it and the resulting deep experiences. In so doing, if we truly realize that nothing is separate and awaken to the principle

석가모니 부처님께서 말씀하시길 육십이견六十二見도 그렇고 삼십이응신三十二應身도 충만하다 하셨는데, 그건 몇 개라고 하는 그 숫자나 이름이 중요한 게 아니라 나의 근본마음을 발견하여 이 세상이 돌아가는 진리를 진정으로 깨달아 과거심過去心, 현재심現在心, 미래심未來心, 이 삼세심三世心을, 이 삼세대천세계三世大千世界를 구분 없이 넘나드는 자유권을 갖는다는 것을 뜻합니다.

그렇게 되면 태양계의 법왕이 될 수도 있고 수많은 달세계와 행성계가 같이 돌아가는 은하계의 법왕이 될 수도 있어요. 그 자료를 가지고 자유롭게 응용할 수 있게 되니 구름과 안개도 내 통신기가 되고, 내 신장神將이 되고, 내 제자가 되고, 모든 게 내가 되어 세상을 평등하게 이끌어 나갈 수 있게 됩니다.

of nondual manifestation, we will become truly and utterly free.

The Buddha once said that the thirty-two manifestations of buddha-nature are all complete and whole, and so too are the sixty-two mistaken views. What this means is that all things work together as one, moving as a whole, without separation. So that when you discover your own fundamental mind and awaken to the truth that sustains this world, you will be able to manifest throughout the universe, one with the minds of all beings of the past, present, and future.

When that happens, you may even become in charge of this solar system, or of an entire galaxy. You will be able to freely apply what you've realized, and clouds and mists will become your messengers, your disciples, and divine protectors. Everything becomes one with you,

모든 게 같이 잘 돌아가게 하려니까 아까 말한 것처럼 주걱으로 내려치듯이 바람도 일으켜지게 되는데 바람이 있어야 체로 쳐지니까요. 이런 일들을 거치면서 더 큰 국난을 면하게 되기도 하고, 또는 더 안타까운 걸 면하게 되는 그런 여건을 갖게 되는 거죠.

빠르게 변하는 세상 속에서 살아남으려면

이런 얘기들이 어떤 분들에게는 허황되게 들릴 수도 있겠습니다. 그런데 지금 현실 얘기도 다 못하는데 내가 그런 허황된 얘기를 하고 있겠습니까? 이건 우리의 생활과 직결된 얘기입니다.

allowing you to guide the world with nondual compassion.

Like the spoon that stirs the porridge, winds will arise to help keep all things moving in harmony. And those winds are necessary because without them, there can be no sifting. By going through these processes, we often avoid even greater suffering, or are spared from national-level hardships or catastrophes.

How to keep up when the world is changing so rapidly

There aren't enough hours in the day to address all of the things that are happening right in front of us. So there's no way I'm going to waste time with empty talk or exaggerations. Everything I've said is true, and directly connected to your day-to-day life.

그러니까 여러분들이 자기의 근본마음을 믿고, 모든 것을 거기에 맡기며 삶으로써, 우선적으로 내 몸과 내 가정을 건강하게 하고 또 사회의 일원으로서 조화롭게 잘 일하는 것부터 실천해 보세요. 그리고 나아가 점점 자유자재할 수 있게끔 해봅시다. 그러다 보면 우주법계의 탐험도 할 수 있습니다. 탐험이라는 것은 몸이 가고 오고 하면서 하는 게 아니라, 내 마음의 거울, 심안心眼으로 본다는 뜻입니다. 근본마음을 통해 모든 게 연결되어 하나로 같이 돌아가고 있으니 진정 그 자리와 한마음이 된다면 가고 옴이 없이 오고 갈 수 있고, 가고 옴이 없이 볼 수 있어 문제를 해결하는데 주걱이 된다 이 소리입니다.

So start by trusting your own fundamental mind and entrusting everything to it. Take the things closest to you – your body and family – and see what you can do to improve them through entrusting. And then continue to experiment with this in your work and daily life.

Keep going forward, experimenting with this entrusting and seeing what you can do to master the ability to use this. In time, you'll even be able to explore the vast universe itself. This exploration doesn't mean traveling physically. It means seeing with the eye of your mind, the mirror-like awareness within.

Since all things are interconnected and function as one through your fundamental mind, if you become truly one with it, you can go here and there without moving, you can see everything everywhere, and you can become the stirring spoon that takes care of what needs to be done.

이 주걱이 **주장자**柱杖子[12]라고도 할 수 있어요. 옛날에는 가르치기 위한 방편으로 주먹을 내밀기도 했고, 지팡이처럼 생긴 주장자를 들기도 했으며, 또 설법을 하고 끄트머리에 선문답 같은 시조를 읊기도 했으나, 지금처럼 빨리 돌아가는 시대에는 걸맞지 않을 수 있습니다. 생활 속에서 실천하고, 실천을 하면서 생각하고, 생각하면서 뛰지 않으면 안 되는, 변천이 아주 빠른 시대에 살고 있습니다. 빠르게 움직여야만 살아갈 수 있는 시대인데 무명옷 입던 시절 타령을 하면 어떻게 되겠습니까? 많이 미비할 겁니다.

---

12. 주장자(柱杖子): 일반적으로 선사(禪師, 스님)들이 좌선할 때나 설법할 때 들고 다니는 지팡이를 말함. 마음공부 과정에서는 안팎에서 일어나는 모든 문제를 내면의 근본마음 한 곳에 맡겨 놓는, 참선 수행을 통해 흔들리지 않는 마음의 중심이 서게 되는 것을 말함.

This spoon can also be seen as a *jujangja,*[18] the traditional staff used by Seon masters. In the past, teachers used their fists or held up their staffs to guide others, and sometimes ended their talks with a profound poem.

But in this rapidly changing age, such methods may no longer be fitting. We live in a time when we have to think while running here and there, and must work on our spiritual practice while dealing with our daily lives. If we try to imitate the ways of a time when people lived without electricity and wore simple hemp clothes, we may find ourselves left far behind and unable to cope.

These days, people wear silk or synthetic fabrics and in all kinds of bright colors. So many things are different now, and they're continuing

---

18. Jujangja(柱杖子): Literally, a monk's staff, but often implied to mean a grasp or reliance upon our fundamental mind.

지금은 누구나 명주옷을 자기 원하는 대로 해 입고 다니는 시대입니다. 많은 것들이 달라졌고 또 지금도 빠르게 변하고 있습니다. 그래서 되도록 사람들이 알아들을 수 있는 말로 가르쳐줘야 합니다. 다양한 재료를 이미 가지고 있으니, 오늘은 이 음식, 내일은 저 음식 해 먹을 수 있는데, 배우지 않으면 그저 빙빙빙빙 돌며 제대로 활용을 못 해 아무 음식도 해 먹을 수가 없어요. 좋은 오븐이 있으면 뭐 합니까? 사용하지 않으면 십 년이 지나도, 이십 년이 지나도 마찬가지입니다.

to change rapidly, so we need to speak in ways that connect with people. With all this change, we have, to give an example, an incredible variety of ingredients in front of us. And having so many new ingredients, there are so many more ways that we can use them to create wonderful meals. But if people don't learn how to use them, they'll just end up going around in circles, stuck in place, unable to make use of the great bounty that lies in front of them. What good is a fine oven if you can't use it? Even after ten or twenty years, it'll still just be sitting there.

So don't just leave this precious foundation of yours sitting idle. Use its capacity to prepare the nourishment you need. When something comes up, respond to it as it is. Respond to the best of your ability, and according to the need. If it calls for a lot of energy, use a lot. If it only needs a little, then use just a little.

그러니 가지고 있는 그 톡톡한 자기의 보배를 그냥 두지 말고 갖추어져 있는 자질과 역량을 마음대로 사용해서 음식을 해 먹으세요. 자기 앞에 닥치면 닥치는 대로, 자기 소용 닿는 대로, 용도대로 전기도 많이 쓸 거면 많이 쓰고, 적게 쓰려면 적게 쓰면서 해 드시란 말입니다.

만약에 전력이 안 보이고 전깃줄만 보이고 전기 들어오는 것만 보인다면 보이는 만큼만 해도 좋습니다. 그러나 전력이 있고 그것이 서로 연결되어 있다는 건 믿으셔야죠. 안 그렇습니까? 애초에 전력이 있고 또 전깃줄로 다 연결되어 있으니까 불이 들어오는 거잖아요. 전구에 불 들어오는 거 뻔히 보면서도 '전력이 있긴 뭐가 있어. 또 뭐가 연결돼 있다는 거야.' 이러면 그다음 얘기는 할 수가 없어요.

Even if you can't see the electricity and can only see the wires or the lights coming on, that's still fine, just work with what you observe. But it's obvious that electricity exists and that it's connected to everything, right? After all, you can see the light bulb turning on, and you know that's happening because of the electricity and wires that bring it from a power station. But if someone sees the bulb light up and still insists, "There's no electricity there," or "None of that stuff is connected together," then there's no point in me trying to talk to them about anything deeper.

Let me say this again: All beings possess Buddha-nature, their fundamental mind, and through this, they are all connected as one, with every aspect of our lives resonating with the whole. This is the utterly profound, fundamental truth that will show you how to grow and

다시 얘기하지만, 모든 것은 불성佛性인 근본마음을 가지고 있으며 이 근본마음을 통해 같이 하나로 돌아갑니다. 당연히 우리 생활도 연결이 되어 있어 서로 맞물려 같이 돌아가고 있지요. 이 진리는 우리 생활뿐만이 아니라 이 세상 돌아가는 모든 거에 기본 지침이 되는 거예요.

생사도 따로따로가 아니라 맞물려 같이 돌아가는 거고, 천당과 지옥도 마찬가지입니다. 이렇게 근본을 통해 하나로 돌아가기 때문에 귀신, 선신이 따로 없고, 중생, 부처가 따로 없고, 여자, 남자가 따로 없고, 동, 서, 남, 북이 따로 없어요.

모두가 이러한 도리를 깨닫고 알아야, 하지 못 한 아픈 역사를 또다시 겪지 않고, 좀 더 발랄하고, 좀 더 위력이 있고, 좀 더 승화시킨 미래 역사를 가져올 수 있습니다. 저는 여러분들이 그렇게 할 수 있으면 좋겠습니다.

develop in your daily life. It is likewise the fundamental truth that directs all the events of this world.

Life and death are not separate events; they are interwoven, unfolding as part of a single, continuous reality. The same holds true for heaven and hell; they are not opposites, but expressions within the same boundless dimension. Because all arises from and functions through this shared root, there is no true division between ghosts and heavenly beings, unenlightened beings and buddhas, women and men, or east and west.

Only by awakening to this truth can we prevent the repetition of painful history. In doing so, we can shape a future that is more joyful, powerful, and spiritually elevated. That is what I sincerely hope for you all.

왜 마음공부를 해야 하나요?

질문자 1(여): 스님, 안녕하십니까? 대구지원에서 왔습니다. 저는 취업 준비생이고 평소에 궁금한 것이 있어 나왔습니다. '참나'와 '거짓 나'는 왜 있는 거며, 그 참나를 계속 지속시키려면 어떤 공부가 필요한지 알고 싶습니다. 그리고 우리는 왜 **마음공부**[13]를 해야 하는지도 궁금합니다.

큰스님: 일단 자기 근본마음이 없으면 육신이 무효예요. 그러니까 육신을 갖고 태어났다는 건 근본마음이 있다는 거죠. 그리고 그 근본마음과 현재 의식이 총동원돼 하나가 돼서 같이 움직이는 게 마음인데, 자기를 있게 한 그 근본마음은 언제나 빼놓고 의식에서 나오는 것만을 마음이라고 하면서 그냥 살고 있어요.

---

13. **마음공부**: 진정한 자유인이 되기 위해 자신의 마음이 어떻게 작용하고 변하는지를 관찰하고 배우며, 그것을 실제 생활 속에서 응용하고 체험해 보면서 알아가는 모든 과정을 뜻함.

Why do we need spiritual practice?

Questioner 1: Hello, I've come from the Daegu branch. I'm finishing college and have had some questions on my mind. Why do both the "true self" and the "false self" exist? What kind of practice is needed to sustain awareness of the true self? And why is it that we must engage in spiritual practice in the first place?

Kun Sunim:[19] Without your fundamental mind, this physical body couldn't exist. So the very fact that you were born with a body indicates that you also have this fundamental mind. This fundamental mind, together with your present awareness, works as one. It moves and functions as what we call "mind." Yet most

---

19. Sunim / Kun Sunim: Sunim is the respectful title of address for a Buddhist monk or nun in Korea, and Kun Sunim is the title given to outstanding nuns or monks.

그리고 사실 세상은 정신계와 물질계가 둘 아니게 돌아가는 데 사람들은 물질세계만 인식하죠. 그러니까 반쪽짜리인 물질세계에서 다시 현재 의식만으로 사는 꼴이 되는 거예요. 제대로 보는 게 하나도 없다는 거죠.

본래 정신계와 물질계가 둘이 아니게끔 돌아가게 돼 있고, 또 자기가 그렇게 하고 있으면서도 근본마음을 뺀 자기가 그냥 하고 있는 걸로 생각해요. 영화배우들이 연기를 자기 마음대로 하는 게 아닌데 말이에요.

people go through life thinking that their present consciousness is who they are, leaving out the very foundation that brought them into being.

In truth, the world operates as one unified reality of both spirit and matter. But people usually only notice the material world. To see even this 50% correctly, they'd need to see it through the eyes of their fundamental mind, combined with the eyes of their present consciousness. But to make things worse, most people are only using their present consciousness, so nothing they see is as it truly is.

It's due to your fundamental mind that the spiritual realms and the material realms are able to function as one. And although people are already living this way, they believe it's their conscious awareness that's doing everything, unaware of the deeper fundamental aspect that is guiding it all. It's like actors thinking they're

보이지 않는 정신계에 감독 같은 일을 하는 참자기가 있고, 그 참자기로 인해 물질세계에 나온 현現 자기가 있어요. 그리고 이 둘은 따로 존재하는 게 아니라 둘 아니게 같이 지금 운용을 하고 있는 거지요. 현재 그렇게 생활을 하고 있으면서도 자기가 그거를 납득을 못해요. 그러니까 납득하기 위해서 공부를 해야겠지요. 보이지 않으니 알기가 어렵겠지만, 내 근본마음이 있음을 알고 전체가 같이 돌아가는 마음 작용을 알아야 합니다. 그걸 모르면 우리는 현시대에, 앞으로 점점 더 살기가 급박해져요.

doing everything on their own, when in fact, there's someone behind the cameras who's directing everything they're doing.

That unseen director is your true self. Because of this true self, your present, visible self is able to exist. But the two are not separate: they are operating together, seamlessly, even right now. Most people don't notice this, though. So to become aware of this, you must study and practice.

It's not easy to grasp what cannot be seen. But you must come to know that your fundamental mind exists, and that all things function together as one through it. Without this understanding, life in today's world will only become more difficult and pressing.

Today's scientific advancements have led to the development of computers, rockets, and all sorts of remarkable innovations. We can look up

지금 과학이 발전되어 컴퓨터가 개발이 되고 로케트가 올라가는 등 이런저런 놀라운 일들이 많습니다. 비행기에 수백 명을 태우고 날아다니잖아요. 하지만 그것보다 더 첨단은 내 마음으로 비행기를 움직이는 겁니다. 이 공부가 바로 그러한 공부예요. 지금 우리가 살고 있는 곳이 중세계인데, 우리가 이 중세계에서 벗어나야 중세계를 굴릴 수 있습니다. 물질계가 진정으로 발전되려면 과학이라는 테두리에 덮여 있는 뚜껑을 열어야 합니다. 뚜껑은 덮여 있기만 한 게 아니거든요. 고정된 게 하나도 없다고 그랬죠? 덮여 있는 과학의 뚜껑을 열어야 진짜 과학이 나올 수 있어요. 자유권의 과학이요.

and see airplanes in the sky all day long, but that technology can be developed even further. It's possible to build planes that fly by mind, and can go anywhere we can think of. Understanding and working with our foundation can be applied to anything.

Right now, we are living in what's called the *middle world,*[20] but we have to be able to step outside of this to truly manage and guide it. For the material world to genuinely evolve, we must go beyond the lid that science has placed over it. There's nothing that's fixed or unchanging. Only by carefully examining this lid and digging into it, can true science emerge. The science that can free people.

---

20. Middle realm(world): In Buddhism, the realm of human beings is sometimes described as the "middle realm" or the "middle world," because it is said to be one of six realms. It exists below the realms of more advanced beings, called devas and asuras, but above the realms of animals, hungry ghosts, and the various hell states.

보이지 않는다고 내 근본마음이 있음을 무시하지 말고, 내 근본마음이 있음을 믿음으로써 둘 아니게 돌아가는 이 마음의 작용을 한 번 경험해 보세요. 벌어지는 일들, 올라오는 생각, 모두를 내 근본마음에 놓고 일단 내 마음이 어떻게 변하는지부터 보세요. 진정한 자유자재권을 얻는 시작이고 정신계와 물질계가 둘 아니게 돌아감을 알 수 있는 시작입니다. 지금 한창 자라는 젊은 세대들이 이 도리를 모른다면, 그래서 이 도리를 아는 사람들이 세계 속에서 드문드문 나온다면 진정한 과학의 발전을 어떻게 이룰 수 있겠어요?

Just because you cannot see it, don't ignore the existence of your fundamental mind. Have faith in its presence, and try experiencing how everything moves as one through it. Whatever happens, whatever thoughts arise, entrust them to your fundamental mind and observe how that changes your inner state. This is the starting point of genuine freedom, and the beginning of realizing that the realms of thought and consciousness, and the material realms, actually operate as one, not two. So the younger generation needs to know this, and deepen their development of it. If the next generation fails to grasp this principle, and there are only a few scattered individuals who get it, how can we ever hope for true scientific advancement in this world?

When I was around twenty years old, I saw flying saucers in the sky on several occasions.

예전에 내가 한 스무 살 즈음에, 비행접시가 하늘에 떠 있거나 날아다니는 걸 여러 번 봤어요. 그 비행접시들이 움직이는 걸 보고 생각이 든 게 뭐냐면 '아, 저 비행기들은 마음으로 자유자재로이 움직이는구나.'였어요. 그러나 아직 정신계와 물질계가 하나가 되어 같이 돌아가는 그런 과학에 도달하지 못한 우리는 그 세계를 가늠해 볼 수도 없고, 그러니 당연히 점프를 해서 넘어볼 수도 없는 거죠. 여러분들은 무언가를 마음으로 자유로이 한다는 걸 어렵게만 생각하는데 이것을 풀어나가는 것이 그렇게 어려운 건 아니에요.

이 마음은 체가 없어서 저 우주 세계를 가는 것도 한 찰나예요. 그러니 심안을 갖는다면 바로 요기를 내다보는 거나, 여기 앉아서 자기 집을 내다보는 거나, 저 먼 우주를 내다보는 거나 똑같아요. 지금 돌아가는 것을 볼 수 있다는 거죠. 마음은 시공을 초월하기 때문에 그래요.

Sometimes they were hovering, and sometimes they were soaring across the heavens. As I watched them zoom around, it occurred to me that, "Ah, those flying craft must be flown by mind." But we, who have not yet reached the point where spirit and matter function as one, cannot even begin to analyze that world, much less leap into it.

People tend to think that doing something freely through our fundamental mind is incredibly difficult. But untying that knot, unlocking that ability, is not as hard as it may seem.

If you have the mind's eye, if you've become one with everything through your fundamental mind, then looking out into the vast cosmos is no different than glancing at what's right in front of you. It's all the same because mind encompasses all time and space.

내가 보려고 생각을 한다면 볼 수 있다는 말입니다. 이 세상 모든 것들은 근본마음을 통해 서로 연결되어 같이 돌아가고 있기 때문에 그렇습니다.

그런데 보는 것도 도가 아니요, 듣는 것도 도가 아니에요. 마음과 마음이 연결돼서 말하는 거를 듣는다 하더라도 그건 도가 아닙니다. 보는 거, 듣는 거, 남의 속을 아는 거, 어디서 왔는지 아는 거, 또 가고 옴이 없이 가고 오는 것, 이런 걸 다 잘한다 하더라도 그건 도가 아닙니다. 바로 이 **오신통**[14] 가운데는 **누진**[15]이라는 열쇠가 있어요. 오신통 바깥으로 벗어나야, 오신통이라는 진리를 벗어나야, 진리를 굴릴 수 있습니다.

---

14. **오신통(五神通)**: 불교의 육신통(六神通) 중에서 누진통(漏盡通)을 뺀 다섯 가지의 신통(능력), 즉 천안통(天眼通), 천이통(天耳通), 타심통(他心通), 숙명통(宿命通), 신족통(神足通)을 일컬음. 천안통(天眼通)은 보는 사이 없이 볼 수 있는 능력, 천이통(天耳通)은 듣는 사이 없이 들을 수 있는 능력, 타심통(他心通)은 다른 이의 마음을 아는 사이 없이 알 수 있는 능력, 숙명통(宿命通)은 과거 어디로부터 왔는지를 아는 사이 없이 아는 능력, 신족통(神足通)은 한 찰나에 가고 옴이 없이 가고 올 수 있는 능력을 말함.

15. **누진(漏盡)**: 일반적으로 마음이 어떤 대상이나 사물 및 상황에 끄달림으로 해서 일어나게 되는 모든 번뇌가 다 없어진 상태를 말함. 불가에서 말하는 오신통(五神通)에서 벗어나 그걸 자유스럽게 굴릴 수 있는 경지를 이름하여 누진이라 함.

So if you gain the eye of mind, then when you intend to see, you will indeed truly see. All things in this world are connected and operate together through our fundamental mind. This is why such seeing is possible.

But even seeing is not the path forward. Hearing is not the path. Even if you can listen in to people who are speaking mind to mind, that isn't the path. Seeing, hearing, perceiving someone's thoughts, knowing their past life, or coming and going without moving – none of these are a path forward, no matter how well you can do them. You must free yourself from and step beyond these powers, beyond even the truths they reveal, and in so doing, when you are truly free of them, you will be able to use them compassionately, as needed.

댁이 나한테 이 공부는 왜 하는지 그걸 물었죠? 공부는 그러기 때문에 하는 거예요. 나를 완전히 알아야 나를 벗어나 자유자재할 수 있으니까요. 그래서 참나인 내 근본마음을 알라는 겁니다. 그 근본마음에 모든 걸 놓았을 때 마음의 작용과 변화되는 것들을 관찰하면서 다시 또 근본마음에 되 놓으세요. 그러다 보면 스스로 진화되어 자신의 차원이 달라집니다.

금방에 금이 모이고 무쇠 전에 무쇠가 모이듯 사람들도 비슷비슷한 생각을 내고 비슷비슷한 마음을 갖고 있는 사람들끼리 어울립니다. 누가 이리로 가라 저리로 가라 하지 않아도 스스로 그렇게 모이게끔 돼 있어요.

You asked me, "Why do we need to practice?" The reason is simple: by fully knowing yourself and your foundation, you'll gain true freedom.

That is why I tell people to let go of everything to their fundamental mind, and then observe and see what changes happen to their perceptions, mental states, and the world around them. And then, they need to keep letting go of those perceptions and understanding as well. As you keep doing this, you will naturally evolve, and your spiritual level, your spiritual awareness, will begin to shift.

Just like gold gathers with gold, and iron ends up with iron, people naturally gravitate toward others with similar thoughts and hearts. No one tells them where to go or whom to gather with; it simply happens on its own.

This is a law of nature, and it is also a law that influences our lives. When you come to know

이 자연의 법칙이 그대로 우리들의 생활의 법칙이에요. 그러니 내가 나를 알면, 다시 말해 나를 있게 한 내 근본마음과 또 내 마음의 움직임을 알게 되면 내가 왜 이러고 사는지 알 수가 있어요. 내가 나를 잘 알면 뭔가 어려운 일이 닥쳐도 좀 더 지혜롭게 일을 풀어갈 수 있고, 그렇게 지혜가 쌓이면서 내 마음의 차원도 높아집니다. 그래서 예로부터 여러 성인들이 말씀하셨죠. 나부터 믿고 나부터 알라고요. 나를 모른다면 이 우주의 섭류를 모른다고도 했습니다. 나를 모르고 어떻게 하나로 같이 움직이는 상대적 원리를 알 수 있겠습니까? 그러니까 우선 나의 그릇을 먼저 만들어 놓고 같이 돌아가는 큰 에너지를 잘 받아서 갖은 용도로 잘 활용해서 써라 이런 얘기예요. 그러니 공부해야겠죠? 알아야겠죠?

yourself – that is, the thoughts and feelings you have, together with this fundamental mind that gave rise to you – you will begin to understand why your life is the way it is.

With a clear understanding of yourself, then even when difficulties arise, you'll be able to face them with wisdom. As that wisdom continues to accumulate, your inner state will gradually rise to a higher dimension.

That is why sages throughout history have said, "Believe in yourself. Know yourself." For if you don't know yourself, how could you possibly understand that everything in the universe is connected together? If you don't know yourself, how could you grasp the truth that all things respond to, react to, and change each other? So, to put it simply, you have to first build your own bowl. Then you'll have something with which to receive and make use of this great energy.

가족을 돕는
진정한 방법

질문자 2(여): 제가 이 자리에 나온 것은 제 동생을 위해서입니다. 제 동생이 지금 병원에 입원해 있거든요. 그런데 의사 선생님들 얘기로는 불과 몇 개월밖에 살 수 없다고 합니다. 제가 동생을 살릴 수 있는 길은 없는지요? 제가 동생을 위해서 어떤 일을 해야 하는지, 스님의 가르침 부탁드립니다.

큰스님: 모든 사람들의 마음이 다 한마음으로 뭉치면 동생을 살릴 수 있겠죠. 음식을 해주는 사람의 마음, 간호해 주는 사람의 마음, 또 의사와 환자의 마음도 전부 다 요.

It's so we can use this as needed that we practice entrusting and experimenting with the energy of our foundation.

How can I help my sister?

Questioner 2: The reason I came here today is because my sister is currently hospitalized. The doctors have told us that she only has a few months left to live. Is there truly no way to save her? Is there anything I can do for my sister? Please, Kun Sunim, I humbly ask for your help.

Kun Sunim: If the hearts of everyone involved could come together as one, then yes, it may be possible to save your sister. The heart of the person preparing food, the heart of the nurse providing care, and the hearts of both doctor and patient: every one of them matters.

이렇게 아플 때 병원에 가는 것도 법이고, 안 가는 것도 법이라고 하는데, 그게 다 이 마음들이 문제이기 때문이에요. 예를 들어, 병원에서 "너 암이다." 이러면 우선 환자들이 이미 죽는 줄 알거든요. 마음으로 '나는 죽었다. 이젠 죽었구나.' 이래요. 그리고 식구들도 그런 생각들을 해버려요. 그러니까 죽는 거예요. 정말 그래요.

그러니까 환자 본인이 우선 암이다, 암이 아니다, 이런 거에 개의치 말고, '그래, 죽이는 것도 너고 살리는 것도 너다.' 하면서 그냥 한군데로 몰아넣고 가야 돼요. 그리고 환자를 보조하는 모든 사람들도 그와 같이 다 한마음으로 뭉치면 살 수도 있죠.

When you don't feel well, going to the hospital could be the correct choice, and not going to the hospital could also be correct. Both are the path. Either is appropriate when viewed through the aspect of what we call "mind" or "heart."

Take, for instance, when a patient hears a diagnosis like, "You have cancer." What usually happens is that the instant they hear those words, they start thinking they're already dead. In their heart, they think, "That's it. I'm finished." And their family also begins to think the same way. And so they die. Really, this happens.

So the patient, first and foremost, must stop being swayed by whether they have cancer or not. Instead, they must say to themselves, "It is you who kills, and it is you who gives life." And then they should gather everything they've worried about and let go of it all to this one place, their foundation. If everyone around the patient,

여기 이 자리에 모인 사람들 중에도 그런 병을 극복하고, 지금까지 괜찮게 살고 있는 분들이 많아요. 자기를 있게 하고 이끌어주는 자기의 근본마음을 믿는 마음이 깊고 강해서 거기에 다 맡기니까, 또 주변의 모든 사람도 그렇게 이끌어 주니까 그 사람이 살 수 있는 거죠.

those who are helping and supporting them also comes together as one, sincerely hoping for their well-being, then yes, it's possible that the patient will recover.

Even among the people gathered here today, there are many who have overcome illnesses and are now living well. It's because they had deep and unwavering faith in their fundamental mind, which gave them life and leads them. They entrusted everything to it. Those around them, moved by this same spirit, also supported them by entrusting their situation to this *one mind*.[21] That's how healing becomes possible.

---

21. One mind(Hanmaum [han-ma-um]): From the Korean, where "one" has a nuance of great and combined, "mind" is more than intellect, and includes "heart" as well. Together, they mean everything combined and connected as one. What is called "one mind" is intangible, unseen, and has no divisions of time or space. It has no beginning or end, and is sometimes called our fundamental mind. It also means the mind of all beings and everything in the universe connected and working together as one.

낫고 안 낫고 그런 거는 내가 어떻게 해줄 수가 없습니다. 내가 의사도 아니고, 또 의사라도 백 퍼센트 다 의사 몫이 아니에요. 만약 의사가 해야 할 역할이 40%라면 본인들이 해야 할 역할은 60% 이상이에요. '아휴, 그까짓 것 아무리 해보면 뭘 해? 이제 죽는다는데 기다리고나 있을 뿐이지.' 그러면 죽는 거예요. 자기 마음이 죽는다고 생각했기 때문에 죽는 거죠.

그러니까 관하는 것도 평상시에 가르쳐 줘야 해요. '지금 우리 집은 모두들 괜찮으니까.' 하고 평소 공부하는 걸 등한시하지 마세요. 사람이 살다 보면 어떤 일이 생길지 몰라요, 갑자기 다리가 끊어져서 사람들이 죽듯이 말입니다.

Whether someone recovers isn't something I can control. I'm not a doctor. Even doctors can't completely control the outcome.

It's often the case that doctors can help people with no more than about 40% of the problem. The remaining 60% or more is in the hands of the patient. But if someone just says, "What's the point of entrusting now? I've already been told that things are bad. There's nothing left but to wait to die," then of course, they'll die. They die because their mind has already accepted death.

That's why we must teach our loved ones about entrusting everything to their fundamental mind, and then observing how things go. Don't let your daily practice slide just because everything seems fine with your family right now. Life is unpredictable. You never know when something might happen, with lives lost in an instant.

내가 여러분들에게 마음공부를 가르치는 것은, 나를 위해서, 여기 오게 하기 위해서, 돈 벌기 위해서 그런 게 아닙니다. 여러분들 자신이 좀, 덜 고통받으며 살 수 있는 거니까, 자기 근본을 믿고 자기 삶에 활용해 보라는 겁니다. 그렇게 미리미리 관하는 도리를 배워서, 일상생활을 할 때 관하면서 살다 보면, 사고당할 수 있는 것도 피해 갈 수 있습니다. 잘 생각해 보세요. 그런 일들이 종종 있습니다. 자기의 근본마음인 주인공이 벌써 알고, 자기를 이끌고 갈 때 위험하지 않게 이끌고 가거든요. 원래 그래요.

The reason I teach people about this practice of entrusting all things to our foundation, Juingong, isn't for my own sake. It's not to draw lots of people here, nor is it to attract donations. I do this because this path can help you live with less suffering.

I'm trying to encourage people to experience their own true foundation and then apply that understanding to their daily life. When you live each day entrusting what you're experiencing to your Juingong, your fundamental mind, you'll find that dangers and misfortunes often quietly pass you by.

You should know that there are actually many times when this has happened to you, but you were unaware of it. Your inherent mind, Juingong, already knows what's going on, and leads you safely forward. Truly.

그러니까 애들이 어리더라도 미리미리들 알려주세요. 하다못해 감기가 들더라도 "너 감기 낫게 하는 거 네 주인공밖에 없다. 네 주인공한테 다 맡겨." 이렇게 자꾸 알려주다 보면 은연중에 어린애들이 조금씩 체험을 하게 됩니다. 그리고 마음이 순수해서 어른보다도 나아요. 그렇게 자기 일들을 자기가 해결하고 나가다 보면 자연스레 제 밥 챙겨 자기가 먹고 살게 되는 거죠. 어른이 가르치기에 달려 있어요. 그렇지 않으면 어른이 돼도 늘 부모가 챙겨줘야 돼요.

중들 얘기를 해 볼게요. 부처님 밥도 그대로 내 밥이 되어 내가 먹을 수 있어야 중들이 제대로 공부하는 거지요. 부처님 밥을 그대로 내려 먹는다고 생각한다면, 그거는 자기 밥을 자기가 먹을 수 없다는 겁니다. 이 말이 무척 뜻이 깊은 말이에요.

That's why we must teach this way of entrusting all things to our children. If they catch a cold, tell them, "Only your Juingong can truly heal you. Entrust everything you're going through to your Juingong." If you continue to remind them like this, they will begin to experience it for themselves. And because their minds are still pure, children will often take to this more easily than adults. As they grow, they will come to handle their own lives naturally and learn to live responsibly. But whether that happens depends entirely on the adults who guide them. If not, they'll grow up needing their parents to look after them.

In the case of sunims, they have to make the Buddha's rice their own rice, then they can eat it. That is to say, they have to become one with whatever comes from buddha. Then it becomes truly theirs, and they are on the correct path of practice. If they just try to get by on the results of

질문자 2: 병에 대해서 지금 동생은 모르고 있거든요. 그냥 몸이 허약해져서 병원에 입원해 있는 걸로 알고 있습니다.

큰스님: 그러게, 그전에도 내가 누차 얘기했었는데, 동생에게 안 가르쳐줬어요? 미리미리 가르쳐줬으면 좋잖아요? 지금 여기 계신 분들도 자녀들에게 자기 주인공을 믿고 모든 걸 맡기라고 미리미리들 가르쳐 주세요. 자기가 스스로 해 나가게끔 하면 그런 불편한 사고는 없을 거 아닙니까?

other's virtue and merit, then none of that will truly be their own. None of it will truly sustain them. There are so many deep implications that revolve around this point.

Questioner 2: My sister doesn't know what's going on with her illness. She just thinks her body has weakened a bit and that's why she was admitted to the hospital.

Kun Sunim: That's exactly what I was talking to someone else about earlier. Wouldn't it have been good if someone had taught her earlier? Everyone here, please teach your children about their Juingong and to entrust everything to it. If they learn early on to take charge of their own lives in this way, then many such unfortunate complications can be avoided.

We can't see them, but do you have any idea how many germs and viruses are out there?

지금 보이지 않지만 얼마나 많은 세균들과 바이러스들이 있는 줄 알아요? 내 몸 안에도 내 몸 밖에도 허다하거든요. 집 안에 주인이 집을 오랫동안 비워두면 함부로 아무나 막 드나들게 됩니다. 들어왔다 나갔다 하면서 말이에요. 친구들을 막 끌어들이면서 집을 망가뜨린다고요. 이 뜻을 알겠어요?

앞서에 얘기해 드렸죠? 가설이 돼 있으니까, 이미 동생과 근본마음으로 다 연결이 돼 있으니까, 동생의 마음까지 불이 들어오게 자기 주인공을 믿고 열심히 맡겨두는 실천을 해보세요.

공부하면서 늘 충만감을 느껴야 하나요?

질문자 3(남): 큰스님, 감사합니다. 광주지원에서 올라왔습니다. 큰스님의 가르침으로 법회 자리에 앉을 때마다 조금씩이지만 마음이 달라지는 것을 스스로 느낍니다. 그것만으로도 저는 상당히 감사합니다. 그리고 개인적으로 큰스님을 이렇게 가까이 뵙게 돼서 무척 기쁩니다.

They're all around us, inside and outside of our bodies. If the owner of a house leaves it empty for a long time, strangers will start wandering in without permission. They'll even bring their friends, and before long they'll end up trashing the house. In this case, the house is your body.

Like I said before: you and your sister are already inherently connected. You're connected through this fundamental mind, so you can help brighten the light within her by wholeheartedly trusting in your own Juingong and letting go of everything to it.

Why does thls radlant awareness fade away?

Questioner 3: Thank you, Kun Sunim. I've come from the Gwangju branch. Every time I sit in a Dharma talk like this, I can feel, even if only a little, that my awareness is deepening, and I owe

저희 가문의 영광인 거 같습니다. (대중 웃음) 여기 계신 모든 분이 저와 같은 마음이겠지만, 비슷비슷한 질문들을 많이 받으실 텐데도 항상 이렇게 자세히 일러주시니 너무 감사드리고 뭐라 표현할 말이 없습니다.

그런데 큰스님께서 그렇게 고구정녕苦口丁寧 일러주시는데도 제대로 못 해 나가는 걸 보면, 제가 약간 게으른 거 같습니다. 그래서 질문하면서도 마음에 걸리긴 하는데 오늘은 이걸 좀 여쭤보겠습니다.

저의 약점이랄까, 이 공부를 해 나가다 보면 아주 충만할 때가 있어 가지고, 평상시 잘 안되는 부분도 조금은 이치가 보이는 거 같고, 이렇게 하면 되지 않을까 하는 생각이 들 때가 있습니다.

that entirely to your teachings. For that alone, I'm deeply grateful.

On a personal note, I feel incredibly honored to be able to see you up close like this today.

I'm sure everyone here feels the same way, but even though you must hear many similar questions again and again, you always answer each one with such care and detail. I'm so grateful. There are no words to fully express it.

Still, even with all the sincere and compassionate guidance you give us, I often find myself unable to truly follow through. So I think I must be a little lazy. Even as I ask this question, I feel a bit hesitant, but I'd like to ask about this anyway.

There are moments in my practice when I feel filled with something deep and radiant. At such times, even things I usually struggle with seem to become clearer, and I get a sense of the best

그럴 땐 제가 잘해 나갈 거 같은 생각이 드는데, 그러다가도 또 힘이 떨어지고, 그러면 마음이 좀 허덕이고 그렇습니다. 그 원인은 무엇이며 그리고 그렇게 충만한 상태를 계속해서 유지해 나가야 되는지에 대해서도 궁금합니다.

큰스님: 우리가 잘되는 것만 있고 안되는 것이 없다면 진리가 아니에요. '잘된다, 안된다'라는 게 상대적인 거거든요. 같이 하나로 돌아간다는 거 자체가 모든 게 한 방향으로 움직인다는 뜻이 아니라 서로 상대성을 갖고 같이 움직이는 거예요.

그러니까 마음을 좀 더 넓게 써봐요. 우리가 차를 타고 갔다 하면 어딘가에선 꼭 내려야 되죠. 내렸다가 또 타고 그래요. 만약 자기 기준에 잘되는 것만 있다면 세상은 돌고 도는 게 아니겠죠.

way to handle them. It feels like I'm finally on the right path. But then, just as suddenly, that energy fades, and my mind begins to flounder again. What causes this? Because it seems like this state of fullness is where I should be all the time.

Kun Sunim: If things always went well and never went wrong, that wouldn't be the truth. Why? Because what's called "well" and "not going well" are already flowing aspects of the whole. When I say everything moves together as one, it doesn't mean that all things move in a single direction labeled "good." It means they move together, as an interacting whole.

So try to use your mind more broadly. Think of it this way: when you take a ride in a car, there always comes a point when you have to get out. And then, sometime later, you'll get back in again. If things only ever went according to your

여러분들의 마음 차원에 의해서 잘되는 것이 있고, 중간치가 있고, 안되는 게 있어요. 그래서 세상 모든 일에는 자기 마음에 따라 차원이 달라지면서 하下로 사는 사람, 중中으로 사는 사람, 대大로 사는 사람이 있는 겁니다. 하지만 그러한 마음의 차원은 고정된 게 아니니 내 마음을 잘 둥글려 가면서 사세요.

광주에서 버스 타고 왔죠? 여기서 볼일 다 보고 나면 다시 여기서 버스 타고 광주로 내려갈 거 아니에요? 종점과 시발점이 둘이 아닌 겁니다. 그러니 잘되는 거, 안되는 거에 대한 고정관념을 갖지 마세요.

idea of "going well," then this world wouldn't be a living, breathing place.

Depending on the level of your own mind, there are things that go smoothly, things that linger in the middle, and things that don't go your way at all. In this world, there are people who live and function at a lower level of mind, those who function at a middle level, and some who function at a very high level of mind. And they live accordingly. But remember: those levels aren't fixed. If you use your mind broadly and harmoniously, the level of your functioning will improve.

You came here from Gwangju by bus, didn't you? And once you've finished what you came for, you'll get on a bus and head back to Gwangju. The ending point is also the starting point. They're not separate things that you should cling to fixed ideas about. The same is true for what's going well and what's not.

'아하, 잘 안되는 것도 나를 가르치기 위해서구나. 안되는 것도 거기서 나오는 거, 되게 하는 것도 거기서 나오는 거다. 안 되게 하는 것이 바로 되게 하는 것이고, 되게 하는 것이 되게 하는 것이다.' 이렇게 한 번 생각해 보세요.

이렇게 생각을 하고 모든 걸 다 근본마음에 되놓아보아요. 여러분이 이렇게 하면 그 생각이 굴려져 바깥으로 나옵니다. 그러면 엉키고설킨 것도 내 한생각으로 풀 수가 있어요. 벌어지는 일들은 마음이 시작이라 마음으로 풀어야 합니다. 물질이 아니기 때문에 물질적으로 엉킨 거를 풀듯이 하려고 하면 안 돼요. 물질 엉킨 거는 내 근본마음에 잘 관하면서 거기에 맞는 노력을 또 같이해야겠죠.

Instead, think like this: "Ah, even what doesn't go well is here to teach me. Whether something works out or doesn't, both arise from the same source. That which prevents something from happening is also what allows it to happen. And that which brings things about is also the same place."

Try viewing it like this, and return everything to your fundamental mind. What you entrust there will change and then come back out. Even tangled, complicated situations can begin to smooth out when entrusted like this. Because everything that unfolds begins with mind, mind is where the solution must start. It's not something material, so don't immediately try to focus on material methods to untangle it. Even for those problems that seem to require your body and effort, start by entrusting them completely to your fundamental mind, and then make the necessary efforts to deal with them.

지혜롭지 않게 마음으로 지은 건 죄업[16]이 됩니다. 인과성으로 오고, 세균성으로 오고, 영계성으로도 오고요, 반복되면 유전성도 됩니다. 이렇게 벌어지는 일들은 마음에서 시작된 거니 마음으로 풀어야지 딴 걸로는 도저히 안 돼요. 독 안에 들어서 벗어날 수 없듯이, 꼭 당하고야 말죠. 그러니까 모든 거를 자기의 근본마음, 주인공에 놓으라는 겁니다. 내 근본마음은 용광로 같아서 모든 걸 녹이고, 또 자가 발전소 같아서 에너지를 만들며, 컴퓨터 같아서 입력하는 대로 새롭게 내놓습니다.

16. 업(業): 몸과 입과 뜻으로 짓는 일체의 행위.

Everything you create through your mind produces effects. When you use your mind unwisely, it creates pain and suffering that will return to you. It may come from the outside, it may come from the inside, it may come as problems with microbes, or it may even come as problems caused by ghosts.

If you keep repeatedly using your mind poorly, that will become something that will affect even your children and their children. All of this started from mind, so that's where we have to begin as well. This is the only thing that can help us.

Sometimes, these problems make us feel like a mouse that's fallen into a giant clay pot. We're just stuck there, sliding back down every time we try to get out. This is why I tell you to entrust everything to your fundamental mind, to Juingong. It's like a furnace that melts every-

그래서 팔자 운명은 없다고 하는 거구요. 모든 것은 마음먹기에 달린 거거든요. 그렇더라도 그게 그렇게 쉽게 되는 게 아니라서 주인공에 맡긴 후에는 인내를 갖고 지켜보고, 또다시 맡기고 지켜봐야 돼요. 그 얽히고설킨 업보가 하루아침에 싹 다 없어지는 게 아니거든요. 차곡차곡 입력이 됐던 것이 하나씩 나올 때마다 내 근본마음에 되놓으면서 지켜보고, 또 새로이 입력하고, 그렇게 하다 보면 앞서 입력됐던 게 하나하나 없어지는 거죠.

thing down. It's like your own power plant that produces infinite energy. It's like a computer that will output something new once you change the input.

Because mind can function like this, we say there's no such thing as fate or destiny. Everything depends on how you use your mind. Still, it doesn't happen just because you think about it. You have to actually try to let go and entrust whatever it is to your Juingong, and then you must observe patiently, taking what comes back out and entrusting it again, while continuing to be aware of what's happening within and without. Karmic entanglements that have been created over years or eons don't just disappear overnight.

As each one reappears, layer by layer, entrust it into your fundamental mind and observe. As you input these one by one, they begin to dissolve, one by one.

그러니까 욕심을 내지 말아요. 대번에 어디 하늘에서 뚝 떨어지는 것도 아니고, 한꺼번에 싹 없어지는 도깨비 장난처럼 그렇게 되는 게 아니에요. 자기가 만든, 이 얽히고설킨 거를 제거하려면 하나하나 인내를 가지고, 믿음을 가지고 꾸준히 해야 돼요. 조금도 허탈히 마음을 먹지 말고 오직 내 근본마음, 이 하나를 굳게 믿고 일체를 놓아야 합니다. 모든 게 들고 나는 곳이에요. 그 자리는 모든 게 무無로 돌아가는 자리입니다. 여기에 편의에 따라 여러 가지 이름을 붙이는 것도 하나의 방편이지요. 들고 나는 모양새 때문에 내가 털구녕이라고도 하고 지금 시대에 맞는 방편으로 컴퓨터라고 부르기도 해요. 말하자면 그렇다는 겁니다. 이 오신통이 컴퓨터같이 일하거든요.

So don't be greedy. Nothing just falls from the sky. And it doesn't all vanish at once like some goblin's illusion. If you need to clear away what you yourself have tangled up, you must be patient, deeply trust your foundation, and go forward one by one. Don't let yourself become discouraged. Deeply trust this wholeness that is your foundation, and take every single thing and return it there.

Everything arises from and returns to your Juingong. It is the place where everything functions together nondually. Because it encompasses everything, it can have any kind of name. Because it's a gateway through which all things flow in and out, I sometimes call it a pore, like the tiny openings in your skin. Sometimes I call it a computer, because this vast spiritual power works the same way: whatever you input into it is processed and returns accordingly.

아까 그러셨죠? 공부하다 보면 충만할 때가 있고 허탈해지기도 한다고 말이에요. 이 세상이 운행되는 것도 높고 낮음이 있기 때문에 모두 질서가 지켜지고 그래서 사람이 살아요. 길고 짧은 게 있기 때문에 질서가 지켜지는데 이건 진리예요. 우리가 마음공부를 해서 쓰자 하면 길고 짧은 게 없는 이 평등한 공부를 하면서 평등치 않은, 길고 짧은 거를 다스려 나가는 거죠. 이 공부가 얼마나 평등한지 알아야 합니다. 공부를 해 나가다 보면 그 평등함 속에서 둘이 아니게 중용을 한다는 사실을 알게 될 거예요. 내가 큰 데 들어가면 크게, 작은 데 들어가면 작은 게 돼 주면서 말이에요.

Earlier, you mentioned that sometimes you see things very clearly and your practice seems to go well, and yet at other times, you feel hollow and listless. But it's because there are highs and lows that this world is able to function. The highs and the lows and the short and the long are what enable us to live. These are what bring forth order.

However, our inherent foundation has no such divisions, so it's able to encompass and fully respond to anything. Thus, when we work at entrusting the events of our day-to-day life, we gradually become able to handle these highs and lows with equanimity. That's the power of this path, for this foundation encompasses all dualities. When you enter a huge situation, you become huge. When you enter a small one, you become small. You harmonize and respond without resistance.

석가모니 부처님께서는 "일체 만물만생이 모두 나 아님이 없느니라." 했어요. 그렇기 때문에 소를 건지기 위해 필요하다면 소 안에 들어가 소가 될 수 있고, 돼지도 될 수 있고 말도 될 수 있습니다. 원하는 자의 마음에, 그 마음의 그릇에 맞춰줄 수가 있어요.

그러다 보니 부처님께서는 돼지가 됐다, 소가 됐다, 여자가 됐다, 남자가 됐다, 애가 됐다, 늙은이가 됐다, 또는 새가 됐다, 곤충도 됐다 하면서, 아니 되는 게 없어요. 자유롭게 나투는 거죠.

The Buddha once said, "Among all living beings and all phenomena, there is not a single one that is not myself." And because of that, if it was necessary to save a cow, he could enter the cow and become the cow. He could become a pig, a horse, or whatever was needed. He could respond to the hearts of others according to the shape of their vessel.

And so the Buddha became a pig, a cow, a woman, a man, a child, an old person. He became a bird and even an insect – there was nothing he could not become. He manifested freely.

So don't be disheartened just because things don't seem to be going the way you want. Don't dwell on whether something is lasting a long time or a short time, or whether something is working or not. What doesn't work is also you doing it. And that, too, is a method to teach both

그러니까 일이 뜻대로 되지 않는다고 낙담하지 마세요. 길고 짧은 거를 생각하지 말고 안되는 것도 내가 하는 거고, 또 그게 다 양면의 가르침을 주기 위한 방편임을 알아, 내가 나한테 감사해야 해요. 그런데 안 되는 일이 있다고 '아이고! 내가 한다고 했는데 안 되는 것도 있더라.' 이러면 안 되겠죠. 안되는 것도 되는 거고 되는 것도 되는 건데 말이에요. 그런데요, 안되는 게 없으면 우리가 이런 이치를 배울 수가 없답니다.

질문자 3: 게으름 피우지 않고 열심히 노력하겠습니다.

큰스님: 그래 봐요. 그리고 한 가지, 아까 "스님, 참 감사합니다." 그랬는데, 감사한 마음이 들더라도 내 모습을 보고 감사하다고 그러지 말아요. 당신 그림자가 내 그림자를 보고서 반가워하는 격이나 마찬가지예요.

sides of the path. So actually, you should be thankful to yourself.

But if you say, "I tried entrusting but it didn't work," this isn't the right way to think. What doesn't work is still working. And what works…, well, that's working too. But without things that don't work, we'd never learn these deeper truths.

Questioner 3: I'll go forward entrusting like this!

Kun Sunim: Keep going just like that. And one more thing, earlier, you said, "Kun Sunim, thank you so much." Even if you feel grateful, don't attribute that to this lump of flesh I'm carrying around. This is just your reflection smiling at my reflection – they're all reflecting the same thing.

석가모니 부처님께서는 “내 고깃덩어리의 모습을 보고 믿지 말아라. 내 육신을 보고 따르지 말아라.” 이렇게 말씀하셨습니다. “네 모습을 네 모습이라고 하지 말아라.” 라고도 하셨습니다.

이는 모든 육신 속에 자생 중생들이 집합되어 있고 네 육신은 그들의 집이며 너는 그러한 너의 심부름꾼이자 관리인이라는 말입니다. 그리고 모든 자생 중생들의 마음과 네 마음이 서로 통하면 너, 나가 둘이 아니라는 뜻이죠.

그러니 진정으로 내 근본마음을 믿으세요. 알았죠? 내 근본마음을 믿고 거기에 다 놓고 가다 보면 만물만생이 근본을 통해 둘 아니게 같이 돌아감을 알 겁니다.

The Buddha Shakyamuni said, "Don't believe in my physical shape. Don't mistake this physical form for the important parts." He likewise said: "Don't think of your form as who you truly are."

He was saying this because even one body is filled with uncountable numbers of other living beings. This shape you have is their home, and you're the caretaker, the manager. When your mind and the minds of all the living beings dwelling within you can communicate as one, then there is no question of separation between you. You all are able to truly live as one.

So, place your trust in your fundamental mind. When you entrust everything there and continue walking forward, you will come to see that all beings and all things function together as one through this foundation. So, let me end with this: Don't become too fixated on whether

여기 계신 모든 분들도 잘되고 안되고에 너무 연연해 하지 마시고 꾸준히 정진하세요. 오늘은 이걸로써 마치겠습니다.

things are going well or not. Just keep steadily and sincerely entrusting everything to your foundation.

한마음출판사 출간 도서
Books by Hanmaum Publications

뜻풀이 경전 (한영합본)

- 대행큰스님의 뜻으로 푼 금강경
  The Diamond Sutra: The Great Unfolding

- 만가지 꽃이 피고 만가지 열매 익어 **(iF 디자인 어워드 수상)**
  대행큰스님의 뜻으로 푼 천수경
  A Thousand Hands of Compassion

생활 속의 참선수행 시리즈 (한영합본)
Practice in Daily Life (Korean / English)

1. 죽어야 나를 보리라
   (To Discover Your True Self, "I" Must Die)
2. 함이 없이 하는 도리 (Walking Without a Trace)
3. 맡겨놓고 지켜봐라 (Let Go and Observe)
4. 마음은 보이지 않는 행복의 창고
   (Mind, Treasure House of Happiness)
5. 일체를 용광로에 넣어라 (The Furnace within Yourself)
6. 온 우주를 살리는 마음의 불씨
   (The Spark that Can Save the Universe)
7. 한마음의 위력 (The Infinite Power of One Mind)
8. 일체를 움직이는 그 자리 (In the Heart of a Moment)

9. 한마음 한뜻이 되어 (One With the Universe)
10. 지구보존 (Protecting the Earth)
11. 진짜 통하게 되면 (Inherent Connections)
12. 잘 돼야 돼! (Finding a Way Forward)
13. 믿는 만큼 行한 만큼 (Faith in Action)
14. 병을 고치는 최고의 방법
(The Healing Power of Our Inner Light)
15. 내 안에 의사가 있다구요?! (The Doctor is In)
16. 마음: 최고의 연금술 (Turning Dirt into Gold)
17. 소용돌이 속에서 춤을 (Dancing on the Whirlwind)
18 마음을 편안하게 두고 (Just Set it All Down)
19. 나를 알면 길이 보여요
(Trust Yourself and the Path Appears)
20. 겁내지 않고 당당하게 (The Secret to Living Without Fear)

한글 단행본(Korean)

- 내 마음은 금부처 (상, 하권, CD 포함) 오디오북 및 e북
- 건널 강이 어디 있으랴 (도서 및 e북)
- 처음 시작하는 마음공부 1

영어(English)

- My Heart is a Golden Buddha
- Like Lions Learning to Roar
- Standing Again
- Sharing the Same Heart
- Touching the Earth
- One Mind: Principles

스페인어(Spanish)

- El Camino Interior
- Vida De La Maestra Seon Daehaeng
- Enseñanzas De La Maestra Daehaeng
- Si Te Lo Propones, No Hay Imposibles

중국어(Chinese)

- 《我心是金佛》(간체자)
- 《人生不是苦海》(번체자, 개정판)

베트남어(Vietnamese)

- Không có sông nào để vượt qua (No River to Cross)
- Chạm mặt đất (Touching the Earth)

※위 책들은 오디오북, e북으로도 일부 제공됨

해외에서 출간된 한마음 도서
Other Books by Seon Master Daehaeng

English(영어)

- Wake Up and Laugh (Wisdom Publications)
- No River to Cross (Wisdom Publications)

German(독일어)

- Wie Fließendes Wasser
  (My Heart is a Golden Buddha),
  Goldmann Arkana-Random House, Germany
- Wie Fließendes Wasser – Hörbuch, SAGA/Egmont
- Vertraue Und Lass Alles Los (No River to Cross),
  Goldmann Arkana-Random House, Germany
- Wache Auf Und Lache (Wake Up and Laugh),
  Theseus, Germany
- Umarmt Von Mitgefühl
  (A Thousand Hands of Compassion),
  Theseus, Germany

Spanish(스페인어)

- Ningún Río Que Cruzar (No River to Cross),
  Kailas Editorial, S.L., Spain

Chinese(중국어)

- 《我心是金佛》(Traditional Chinese, Taiwan),
  橡樹林文化出版, Taiwan

Russian(러시아어)

- Дзэн И Просветление (No River to Cross), Amrita-Rus, Russia

Indonesian(인도네시아어)

- Sup Cacing Tanah (My Heart is a Golden Buddha), PT Gramedia, Indonesia

Vietnamese(베트남어)

- Không có sông nào để vượt qua (No River to Cross), Vien Chieu, Vietnam
- Tỉnh thức và cười (Wake Up and Laugh), Vien Chieu, Vietnam
- Chạm mặt đất (Touching the Earth), Vien Chieu, Vietnam

Czech(체코어)

- Probuď se! (Wake Up and Laugh), Eugenika, Czech Republic

한마음선원 본원

경기도 안양시 만안구 경수대로 1282
(석수동, 한마음선원) ㈙13908
Tel: (82-31) 470-3100 Fax: (82-31) 470-3116
홈페이지: https://www.hanmaum.org
이메일: jongmuso@hanmaum.org

국내지원

강릉지원 강원도 강릉시 하평5길 29(포남동), T.(033)651-3003
공주지원 공주시 사곡면 위안양골길 157-61, T.(041)852-9100
광명선원 충북 음성군 금왕읍 대금로 1402, T.(043)877-5000
광주지원 광주광역시 서구 운천로 204번길 23-1, T.(062)373-8801
대구지원 대구광역시 수성구 수성로 41길 76, T.(053)767-3100
목포지원 전남 목포시 백년대로 266번길 31-1(상동), T.(061)284-1771
문경지원 경북 문경시 산양면 봉서1길 10, T.(054)555-8871
부산지원 부산광역시 영도구 함지로 79번길 23-26, T.(051)4033-7077
울산지원 울산광역시 북구 달래골길 26-12(천곡동), T.(052)295-2335
제주지원 제주특별자치도 제주시 황사평6길 176-1, T.(064)727-3100
중부경남 경남 김해시 진영읍 하계로 35, T.(055)345-9900
진주지원 경남 진주시 미천면 오방로 528-40, T.(055)746-8163
청주지원 충북 청주시 청원구 교서로 109, T.(043)259-5599
통영지원 경남 통영시 광도면 조암길 45-230, T.(055)643-0643
포항지원 경북 포항시 북구 우창로 59(우현동), T.(054)232-3163

Anyang Headquarters of Hanmaum Seon Center

Tel: (82-31) 470-3175 / Fax: (82-31) 470-3209

onemind@hanmaum.org   www.hanmaum.org/eng

Overseas Branches of Hanmaum Seon Center

ARGENTINA

(Buenos Aires)

Tel: (54-11) 4921-9286 email: hanmaumbsas@hotmail.com

(Tucumán)

Tel: (54-381) 408-2894

email: tucumantemplohan@gmail.com

CANADA (Toronto)

Tel: (1-416) 750-7943 email: hanmaumtoronto@gmail.com

GERMANY (Kaarst)

Tel: (49-2131) 969551

email: info@hanmaum-zen.de

THAILAND (Bangkok)

Tel: (66) 61-413-7000 email: hanmaumbkk@naver.com

USA

(Chicago)

Tel: (1-224) 632-0959 email: hanmaumchicago@gmail.com

(Los Angeles)

Tel: (1-323) 766-1316 email: hanmaumla@gmail.com

(New York)

Tel: (1-718) 460-2019

email: nyhanmaum@gmail.com

(Washington D.C.)

Tel: (1-703) 560-5166 email: 5gongdc@gmail.com

책에 관한 문의나 주문을 하실 분들은
아래의 연락처로 문의해 주십시오.

한마음국제문화원/한마음출판사

경기도 안양시 만안구 경수대로 1282 (우)13908

전화(Tel): (82-31) 470-3175

팩스(Fax): (82-31) 470-3209

e-mail: onemind@hanmaum.org

hanmaumbooks.org

If you would like more information about these books or
would like to order copies of them,
please call or write to:

Hanmaum International Culture Institute
Hanmaum Publications

1282 Gyeongsu-daero, Manan-gu, Anyang-si,
Gyeonggi-do, 13908,
Republic of Korea

Tel: (82-31) 470-3175

Fax: (82-31) 470-3209

e-mail: onemind@hanmaum.org

hanmaumbooks.org